This Mother's Life

Diary of a Bicultural Working Woman
Who Worries, Dreams, and Loves

Nina Mohadjer

All rights reserved. No part of this book shall be reproduced or transmitted in any form or by any means, electronic, mechanical, magnetic, photographic including photocopying, recording or by any information storage and retrieval system, without prior written permission of the publisher. No patent liability is assumed with respect to the use of the information contained herein. Although every precaution has been taken in the preparation of this book, the publisher and author assume no responsibility for errors or omissions. Neither is any liability assumed for damages resulting from the use of the information contained herein.

Copyright © 2011 by Nina Mohadjer

ISBN 0-7414-6710-0

Printed in the United States of America

Published October 2011

INFINITY PUBLISHING
1094 New DeHaven Street, Suite 100
West Conshohocken, PA 19428-2713
Toll-free (877) BUY BOOK
Local Phone (610) 941-9999
Fax (610) 941-9959
Info@buybooksontheweb.com
www.buybooksontheweb.com

I dedicate this book to my parents, for always encouraging me to write. Even though I'm not sure that they would approve my chosen vocabulary in the following pages. I love you more than words can possibly express. Thank you for everything you have done and still do for me.

To my daughters, for being just the way you are. You are beautiful, and I wish you all the success as you live your lives. You are the reason for my smile; you challenge and sweeten my days simultaneously. I love you more than the universe!

To all my friends who loved my writing style and asked to see a book, thank you for the encouragement.

Nina Mohadjer
May 2011

Contents

Prologue

Characters

The Diary

Prologue

I hate to admit that the idea for this book wasn't originally mine. It came from numerous people who had read my blog and had commented that they loved my writing style. In some ways, the author of this story isn't me but every woman—or, maybe, more precisely *every working mom*.

A woman without children might laugh at that distinction, but as a working mom, I believe that beside men and women, there should be a third category specifically dedicated to us. Only we know how it is to do the splits as we stretch to balance family and work for twenty hours a day. Only a woman who has children *and* a boss can understand how important the micromanagement of every day on the calendar is and how unforeseen events have to be expected and taken into account. Only she will understand how running from a parent–teacher conference to a new policy meeting to a night of intimacy is an everyday task.

Work doesn't mean necessarily work; school can be substituted here. I've experienced both, and at times, I'm amazed I survived.

The characters are all fictitious, but the following pages are a look into one woman's hidden dreams, thoughts, hopes, and expectations, as written in her diary. It isn't autobiographical, and although many of you might recognize you or me in our heroine, be assured that she isn't one specific person. She, and every other character for that matter, is a combination of all of us because every woman is a chameleon, a blending of daughter, wife, mother, employee, employer, lover, and friend. We're a hybrid of all the different roles society has given us.

However, this mix makes us unique, because in all the chaos we might experience on a daily basis, we remain young girls in our hearts. We never forget the original dream and hope we had. It is as Simone de Beauvoir described, "The torment that so many young women know, bound hand and foot by love and motherhood, without having forgotten their former dreams."

We all can find comfort as we watch the heroine wrestle with the exact dilemmas we encounter every day and realize that we have much more in common than we might know.

—Nina

Characters

Amir — *Husband*

Lili — *Daughter*

Yasmin — *Daughter*

Mr. and Mrs. Etemad — *Parents*

Sam — *Brother*

Kate — *Sister-in-Law*

Liz — *Boss*

January 1, 2006

Yes, I know I'll start the New Year by writing on your pages, diary, and promising that I'll be much better about writing every day this coming year. To be honest, I can't believe that I'm actually still writing in a diary. I wonder how many mothers nowadays still have the time to do that? Huh.

New Year Eve went as usual. Lili, Yasmin and I watched a movie, a very good choice staring Julia Roberts. I always tell the girls that I would love to know how wide Julia's smile is. Then we played Monopoly and Pictionary. I always buy too much land and end up loosing. Haha. We had a great dinner, I had made duck and some Persian rice, gobbled up some midnight snacks, and went to bed right after midnight.

Amir, my so-called *husband*, or how I call him now the *father of my children* went to bed much earlier and avoided the kids and me. That's another thing that hasn't changed. Why am I still with him? Maybe it's better to not even remind me. I guess it's a habit—or maybe I just want to believe that something is still there. Sometimes I think men just aren't worth it anyway.

Okay, so I put on my cotton pajamas. Hey, but hiding underneath those cotton PJs is some sexy underwear. It's so funny, Lili and Yasmin make fun of me because I don't do the typical Jockey for Women. I go for the sexy undies. They laugh and tease me, "You have that?" They have no idea that romance used to be a normal part of my life.

So what happened?

Hmm, now that's a good kickstart for this year! Let's celebrate 2006 by trying to uncover the answer.

January 2, 2006

Today it was back to work. The office building is still beautiful in my eyes. Perfect for a graphic art company. Very artistic, with high ceilings, many windows, and unusual architecture. But oh man, I hate those fucking idiots who laugh their fake laughs, pretending they would get it on every night, and then say, "Happy New Year!" I just want to put tons of bars of soap in their mouth to get them to shut the hell up!

Work generally was work; there was more stuff to do than I thought. A couple of the clients were acting up. I guess they either must have had too much to drink over the holidays or didn't get laid.

But then again who does? At least I don't. I can't even remember the last time he glanced in my direction. Maybe we should just not discuss sex. ☺ That's a joke. Actually, it was always a joke.

Of course, when I met him, I thought that lovemaking must be great. (Now I don't even know what it means.) I guess people are so fucked up that they just *do it* like rats—truly the "Wham! Bam! Thank You Ma'am!" approach or, as I call it, the David Bowie method of sex. Now my question is, shouldn't sex/lovemaking be about the togetherness of two people, making them feel closer during it? At least I always used to put his pleasure first. I was always trying new things or coming up with ways to tease him. But after listening to all the women at the lunch tables, I guess everyone is faking it. They have this attitude of if you're good in bed, the guy will love you forever.

Yeah right! Go on and believe it.

Or as my grandmother would say, "If you feed a man well, he will love you forever."

Again, yeah right.

I did both. I have no idea whether I was a Heidi Fleiss in bed or a Wolfgang Puck in the kitchen, but hey, isn't the effort worth something? Look, I have no idea how many girls are born with the *Kama Sutra* in one hand and the *Williams–Sonoma Cookbook: The Essential Recipe Collection for Today's Home Cook* in the other.

That's enough about the way to a man's heart. Anyway, after fixing a couple of the client files, I had cleaned up the holiday mess.

Lunch was the usual crowd. Judy showed off the rock on her ring finger by constantly flipping her hair. As I watched her, I wondered, *When will that bitch notice that her hair is short and doesn't need to be flipped?* You know she must be a cooking Heidi Fleiss. I wonder what she does in bed because her guy is so cute and way too much for her. Of course, if I were his girlfriend, things would be different.

Okay, I have to go to bed now—all alone as usual.

January 4, 2006

Today I had to go to the gynecologist. I guess not having sex for a year has consequences and I told Dr. Rosenstein that I felt like I was going into menopause. She just laughed, which is all doctors do nowadays. They have so many patients, and add to that all the crap with insurance companies, they just see us as files, not people.

But at least she's a woman. Seriously, I can't understand why men become gynecologists. I mean sitting all day between the spread legs of a woman must be great for sex. Or maybe that ruins the attraction when you have to see all different shapes and sizes of down there. Yuck! I'm sure they have to use some kind of medical instrument on their girlfriend or wife first before doing it. You know basically it's a force of habit. Just imagine it: "Hey honey, when was the date of your last period? Maybe I should give you an ultrasound?" Imagine the look on the woman's face. Ha ha ha ha!

Alright, back to reality, my doctor didn't find anything physically wrong, so I was faced with the same questions. *Blah blah blah.* I told her about not having any intimacy with my still-husband or with any other man. She said that what I was going through was normal and that at my age a "healthy sexual life" would be important. I wanted to jump her and say, "First, I would need a lover!" She wanted me to have some blood work done, so I did. I should have the results by the end of next week.

After that I came home, took a shower, and cleaned up the house. The whole time I wondered how the kids do it—destroy the house. I mean it takes me half a day to tidy up, and it takes them only fifteen minutes to mess up the whole house. I mean honestly why does the hairbrush have to be on the kitchen counter? Did you ever hear that there is a place in this house called the bathroom?

Then I called my mother, who told me that my brother's wife, Kate, was having another baby. I'm happy for them, but I wonder why Sam didn't tell me. I'm not sure, but I think I haven't spoken to Kate for two months now. I can't believe I introduced that bitch to Sam. Well, but then again, I shouldn't act all snotty like Amir's family. They always put me and my actions under a magnifying glass. None of them is ever excited about anything I do, achieve and accomplish. As if they are waiting for me to fall, so that they can be happy and say "I told you so!" I'm happy that she's good to my brother, she doesn't have to live with me, and even though I hate to admit it, I could probably learn a lot from her. How on earth does a woman always have a manicure and pedicure; look so toned; bake the best chocolate chip cookies in the county; satisfy her husband, one of the best-looking men in the world; *and* be mother to two little wild boys? She was always well organized. I should hate her, but I don't.

There are some women, who just get everything—the career, the big ring, and the cute man. Every time I talk to my mother, it breaks my heart because I know I must be her biggest disappointment. Poor thing, she doesn't even ask about my marriage anymore. But honestly, what's there to ask? We've been sleeping in different beds for nearly a year and talk only about necessities. How is it possible that such a big love turned out like this? I would really like to move on and initiate a physical separation. And while I would love to focus on my upcoming freedom instead of focusing on all the reasons this marriage didn't work, it is a huge step. And yes, I admit, I'm scared being single again.

I had lunch with my girlfriends Lauren and Julia at the Marseille, and they seem to be doing fine. At least they pretend that they only issues they have are with the television programs their kids watch. You know whether they should be allowed to watch a kissing scene that is more than two seconds long. I pretend to be interested in their conversation all the while thinking, *You've no idea what your kids are doing behind your back. They are out practicing what you think they shouldn't be watching.* My guess is Lauren would freak out if she found out that at the age of 13, her little "Miss Princess" isn't a virgin! I also know who had his fun with her, Ms. Lauren's nephew! She sends her kids to her brother's house, thinking, *Oh, the kids get along so well, and Ali can learn so much from Brianna and Brian.* Well, yeah, she sure did learn a lot from Brian. Of course, maybe it's her way of hinting that she knows but she doesn't want to admit it.

It just shows that you never know what's going on behind the walls of people's homes. If you asked others, they would probably think that I have it all—a nice car, nice house, nice husband, and wonderful kids—but they have no idea! Sometimes I want to scream at all of them. I would love to tell them that I'm planning to get a divorce and that I tried to commit suicide.

But I'm too chicken to do that.

Good night for now.

January 5, 2006

As my girls would say, "Oh my gosh!"

I was invited to this company event, and there was this guy who came up and started talking to me. Sure, I meet many people, but his approach was different. He was talking to *me* and not as a professional. Well, one thing led to another, and during lunchtime he sat down next to me.

I noticed immediately that he was interested not only in my work as a designer, but also in my personal design. I could just tell by the way he looked at me. I guess I'm a woman after all!

He gave me his business card. I'll write him an e-mail because I'm too shy to call.

The bonus to these expos is that during them my boss Liz is so busy trying to impress our clients, that she puts her bitchiness on the shelf and wears her frozen smile. As long as the clients are there, we have a job and she leaves me alone. She can fake it all she wants. At the end, she is the boss and I am her employed graphic artist. As long as I get to do what I am good at, she can do her business.

The event was very good by the way. The graphic artist had some interesting pieces, and I'll definitely research some more of her work. Maybe I could learn some new things to apply to the *Nolan* project.

January 6, 2006

I feel like a teenager again! I can't believe it. I'm thirty-four years old, and I was looking at the card and thinking over and over again about why I shouldn't send him an e-mail. *First,* I thought, *maybe he does want to talk to me about work. We met at a designer meeting after all.* But then I remembered the way he looked at me, the tone of his voice, how he gave me the card, and when he said good-bye. What am I doing? Would it be an affair? Sure, I'm separated, but legally I'm still married, right? Again, I have no relationship to the man in my house and I haven't done anything illegal or unethical with the man whose business card I held in my hand, right?

I was thinking about it the whole day. I couldn't even finish the *Nolan* project, which is due next Tuesday, and Liz was asking about it already. I told her that it would get done all the while thinking about this man. His card read Benjamin Walsh, senior consultant. I wonder what he consults about. With his aura, he could talk about anything, even the latest sale at the supermarket. I would buy just to see him.

I guess I have to stay at work this weekend to finish this stupid project. I love what I'm supposed to do at my work, but this *Nolan* woman is driving me nuts with her constantly changing ideas. She has no clue about design but thinks she should be a professor of advertising!

Okay, back to Mr. Ben. It wouldn't be cheating, right? When you already have a relationship and start another one, that's cheating. Well, the first part doesn't exist in my case, right?

I had to pick up Lili and Yasmin at school today because Lili had to go to lacrosse and Yasmin had a doctor's appointment. In two years Lili will be driving. That'll be good—or maybe not. Sure, she promises me now that she won't drive fast and will pay attention. I'm a mother, so I automatically worry. I think there's probably an adrenaline change—let's call it a "worry twenty-four/seven" hormone—which develops during the nine months of pregnancy and never leaves you until you leave it by dying.

Okay, so I lost track of my day again as I dive into home life. I really hope Yasmin doesn't have the strep throat that has been going around for a while now. And now Lili wants to quit lacrosse because of Erin, this bitchy girl on her team. I kept telling her all the time that she should never give up because of another person. And then I started digging into the story: It turns out that the trainer likes Lili a lot and wants her to be something like a team captain and Erin is freaking out. She stares at Lili the whole time. I told Lili that next time I would hang around the field and stare back at her. I reminded her that Erin comes from a typical never-left-America, nouveau-riche family. Lili always tells me I shouldn't intimidate people, but I think she secretly likes having a feisty mother. This is the best! I remember when I was her age and I loved being liked my mom, but I would never admit it.

Well, maybe I'll write Ben an e-mail after the project is done on Tuesday. He doesn't have my card; otherwise I would sit back and pray for him to send me a line.

January 7, 2006

I had to take the girls to the mall. The post-Christmas and New Year sales just can't be missed. They had some very cute sweaters at Abercrombie.

Then we went to get some shoes. I still can't believe that my girls' feet are bigger than mine. For lunch I got some sandwiches at Subway, which I hadn't had in a long time. I also just love to see how these people try to not get confused as you tell them all the things you want and don't want for three different sandwiches. I wouldn't have the patience for that, and more importantly I would put the wrong things on each sandwich. What a picture!

Amir wanted to go to the movies, but I was too tired from the shopping spree. The girls went with him. I don't think he included me in his invitation anyway. "So, girls, who wants to go to the movies with Daddy?" I mean what kind of question is that. Hello, I'm not your girl, and my daddy is in France.

So I had a relaxing evening at home. I did not have to go to the office this weekend after all, since I was able to get most of the work done on Friday. The rest can be finished on Monday and finally I can breathe again.

January 8, 2006

I did nothing exciting today. It was just laundry and some cleaning up, the usual weekend stuff.

For dinner, Amir, the girls and I went to Laura's house. Good to visit a child-hood friend. It feels as we never grew up. It's so funny that people think we are such a perfect couple. I must be a real good actress and this is a really good charade.

January 9, 2006

I did it! I can't believe it, but tonight after work, the kids were done with homework, the dishes were done, and the laundry was finished, I was all by myself and I wrote *the* e-mail.

It was nothing sexy. I used my personal e-mail; otherwise, Liz might have seen the note. That would be like printing in *The New York Times* because she never knows to keep her nose in her own affairs. I basically wrote him that it was nice meeting and talking to him. I told him I was sorry that I didn't have a card with me, but now he would have my contact information. I made sure I included my cell number under my signature.

Maybe he'll call. At least I'm giving him options.

It's amazing how many men don't like to write letters or e-mails. People always blame it on their more analytical brain, but I think I know the real reason: They just don't want to put in anything in writing and permanently record it. I guess they forget that women have great memories—no matter if it's oral or written.

To get back to the point, I went back and forth about sending the e-mail. It is already as though Amir and I are divorced, so I really shouldn't feel guilty. On the other hand, maybe Ben already has forgotten about me and will never respond.

At work, nothing was new. I'm still working on the *Nolan* project, but it's improving, and I think it's going to be really good. I was talking to Jessica, the girl who works in the cube next to mine and she told me that I was way too good for this job anyway; she said I should get my PhD and start teaching. And this comment comes from one of the best graphic artists in this world! That doesn't sound bad. I just had never thought about it before. I'll call my mom tomorrow morning and see what she thinks. I don't know whether I should go back to school full time and finish my studies or just keep working. So thankful for Jessica! We got along from the very first moment I started my work here. She has helped me to keep my sanity.

Then there's the money issue. I do have some savings, but I could never pay for the whole thing. I would love to go to Westmore University, but they are private and expensive. Based on Amir's income, I couldn't apply for a loan. He wouldn't help me out either. He would rather die! He feels like he has no obligation to me. I wonder where he got that idea. When I was romantic, young, and love-struck with him, he would have offered to help. Maybe I can stay for a couple of more months at this work and save more.

But I wanted to take the summer off in order to visit Europe and Asia with the girls.

Grrr, I'm so tired of thinking. At work I have to think for everyone else, at home I have to think of the girls and the house, and I get so tired when it's finally time to think about myself. It drives me insane.

It's like I came into this world as daughter of Mr. and Mrs. Etemad, became the wife of Mr. Irani, and now am Lili and Yasmin's mother. I wonder where *I* went. I guess I stopped existing.

January 10, 2006

Today was by far the most fucked-up day, you could possibly imagine! I constantly looked around to see whether someone would show up with a hidden camera. I mean, there were so many ridiculous incidents, that it was pathetic! Why does all this shit always happen to me?

First, I spilled a whole pot of coffee on my new white silk shirt and over the countertop. After hearing the commotion Amir came into the kitchen, and instead of helping me, he just looked at me and shook his head.

Then the girls both came and again, no help. They had just forgotten things from last night. "Mom, could you sign this? Can you sign that?" "Where is this? Where is that?" "Did you wash my Abercrombie T-shirt?" You name it! How many times do I have to remind them that they should finish this stuff at night? I think I'll drag this half-broken family to a language therapist because we seem to be speaking in different tongues—or at least they don't understand what I'm saying. But hey, no one would ever admit that mom was right. I guess it's too much fun to hate me or call me the "Evil Lady."

The other day Yasmin was asking me why I enjoyed screaming so much of the time. Her question struck me. I asked her if I was always yelling and screaming, and she just nodded. I told her that my patience level was sometimes at the breaking point several times a day. I could tell that she understood me in that moment, and I think she might have actually felt bad for me momentarily. One day they'll understand me.

At work the *Nolan* project was due. I thought I had finished it until that bitch, the client, came into my office and told me that she had changed her plans about the design she wanted. I mean, are you fucking out of your mind? I had been working long hours and a whole weekend on this while she was having one of her little tea parties! And, of course, I had no support from Liz. She had on her phony smile and nodded like a dashboard doggie. I know if Liz doesn't keep this woman happy, her head will be chopped off. So for her it's more fun to see mine hanging above this woman's mantle as a souvenir. Whatever! I really like Jessica's idea of going back to school more and more. I'm wasting my talents here.

(I have no luck in love and on the job. I guess that's the story of my life.)

I tried to defend myself, but at the end of the day, Liz is the boss, and it always takes an asshole to be the boss, right? And the client is the one paying, so we have to be nice, no matter how demanding she acts.

On my way home some guy, who was using his cell phone while driving, ran into the back of my car. Thank goodness, no one was hurt, but I had to wait for the police and called Amir to ask about the insurance stuff. The whole situation was stupid, but the guy—a total moron for using his cell—was nice though, and at least he apologized.

Once I was at home, Yasmin told me that she refused to go back to school because her math teacher was the meanest woman. When I asked her why, she told me that the woman lectured everyone in front of the class. I was thinking to myself, *Isn't she paid to do that?* Good thing I didn't say that out loud. It turned out the teacher had given them a test, which hadn't turned out well, and instead of looking at her own poor job of teaching, she blamed the kids for not studying. Why do teachers always blame the kids? Come on, when the whole class fails, it must have been on the teacher's side as well, right? I told her that I would work with her on the problem. I think her bad mood might be also the result of her sore throat. Wonder why the doctor's office has not called yet to give us the results. If I don't hear anything by tomorrow noon, I will definitely call them up and find out.

To top off my day, Amir came home in this "great" mood. I guess I'm his dumpster for pissy moods. Instead of calming me down after the accident, he started blaming me. I'm sick and tired of his misogynist statements. He told me that I must not have seen the guy. Well, hello, the guy drove right into my trunk while chatting on a cell. Whatever. I just ate my salad and went straight to bed, but I wanted to jump out of the window!

Great start for a New Year—just fucking great!

And oh, by the way, no news from Ben!

January 11, 2006

I guess I had to have yesterday in order to appreciate today. Today was the best day of my life. Talk about roller coasters. I guess my hormones are accompanying me on this ride! I finished and handed in the *Nolan* project; then I came home, and Amir was there, surprising me with a great dinner and even flowers. He must have noticed the puzzled look on my face. He said he wanted to start fresh and that the past year had been so idiotic. He said that he had missed me and wanted to know if we could call a truce for a while. And typical me, I got so emotional. I started crying and fell right into his arms. I hadn't realized how much I had missed that. I had forgotten how tall he was and how good he smelled. Lili and Yasmin should have been there, and they would have had a yuck attack and called me an "emotionally disturbed person." Good thing they were upstairs in their rooms at that time.

I asked Amir why he had a sudden change of heart. Amir said that on his way to work, he had heard our song and that it had brought back some good memories. He said that we had invested too much into our relationship, and it was still worth fighting for. I think regardless of my recent dislike of him, I still love him. He was the first man in my life after all—and he will always be the father of my children. We still don't have anything else in common, but something must be there.

Anyway, we had a great dinner. He had made my favorite salmon and some salad. He knows how it turns me on when a man cooks for me, so sweet…and then the girls suggested that we should go to the city for the weekend, which will be great because I won't have to work on anything. I haven't been there in a while now.

That night we were still in separate beds. I don't want to rush into anything. Maybe that was the mistake we should have avoided from the very beginning. Who knows? Maybe the old-fashioned way is right: Find your soulmate first and then sleep with him. We decided to take things slow for now, which means basically to start dating again.

Yes, I'm optimistic; I want it to work for myself but mostly for Lili and Yasmin. I always dreamed of having an intact family: father, mother, and kids. I don't want them to be like sixty-seven percent of households that are torn between their parents, spending a weekend here, a weekday there.

But again, the kids are old enough now to see and hear everything. They know that their father and I don't get along. The other day Lili asked me "Why haven't you asked for a divorce yet?". I nearly fell off my chair. I asked her "Don't you want your father and I to stay together?" She said "Well, that would be great, but not realistic, mom! You guys are just so different!"

I asked "Wouldn't you and Yasmin mind being from a broken family?" She just gave me a look and said, "Mom, you have no idea how many of my friends' parents are divorced. It's not that big a deal."

I guess she's right. But at least for now, we decided to try again. Even though I'm strong, I really don't want to be alone. After all, in a couple of years, the girls will be heading of to college and then what?

January 12, 2006

I had to take a half-day today. The results from Yasmin's swab test came back: It's strep. Now we're all back on antibiotics. I hate that stuff!

I told the doc's receptionist to send the prescription to CVS and then went to pick it up. I must not have paid attention because when I got home, the woman at the pharmacy had given me the wrong stuff. I called in because I wanted to see whether they had a driver who could bring me the real medication. When I called, the bitch on the end of the line copped such an attitude. It made me sick. She said that it wasn't their responsibility to check; it was mine. I told her that she should be happy that I hadn't mistakenly given the stuff to my child. She said that I had to return it anyway. Hello, lady, there are seven inches of snow outside—and I don't live right around the corner! I guess I could have called Amir and asked him to pick up the pink fluid on his way home, but it had to be an exact exchange of the medications, and I didn't want another mixup again.

So I had to drive out all the way to the drugstore again. I felt like I was in *Doctor Zhivago*. I was so grateful that my car had four-wheel drive, and I didn't get stuck. As I passed by the Blueman estate, I saw some people—four Hispanic-looking women—were struggling to get their car out of a hole. I couldn't stop to help them. But I did a good deed; I called the police to send someone over to help and gave them an exact location. I guess I'm not such a bad person after all. I got the medicine exchanged and went bad home to my poor sick baby.

Well, Yasmin took the medication and went to sleep. I took a moment to just sit and watch her. She's so cute. On the outside, she wants to behave like a little woman even though she is only twelve years old, but inside she's still my baby. As I watched her sleep, it struck me that she looks exactly like she did in her baby pictures. I remember the moment they put her in my arms. She was like a little angel, so sweet, so little. Oh my gosh, how time passes. I guess those lotions I put on my face at night must be doing a good job to prevent wrinkles so that I forget how old I really am.

I logged into work from home and answered a couple of e-mails. Because my big project is done and the little ones on my desk can be done in a matter of days, Liz hadn't said anything when I had sent her an e-mail that I had to leave.

Sometimes I wonder why she even hired me. I had made it very clear from the very beginning that I had children and they were a priority.

"Sure," she had said, "we are a family-friendly corporation. We encourage working mothers."

Encourage my ass! They find every possible way to give me the evil eye when I have to call in. But what am I supposed to do? Eat my children for a breakfast? Then they won't interfere with the work schedule. Sheesh! You know none of the other women have kids—except Judith—but hers are already in college, so that doesn't count. Why should they care if I take my fifteen vacation days to go to Aruba or to watch my sick child?

The next time I go to a job interview, I'll be very clear from the very beginning that I have children and it may mean I have to take off to take care of them. Take it or leave it. But again, they always say at the beginning how supportive they will be because they know once they get you hooked, it'll take some good luck to hold them to that.

Yasmin should be fine by tomorrow and will be able to go back to school. I bet Liz is praying hard that I'm back.

January 13, 2006

I can't believe it: *He wrote back!* My blood froze this afternoon when I saw his name in my inbox. It was so weird. Of course right then Lili wanted to be on the computer, and so I had to try to hide the e-mail. Very funny! I felt like I had been doing something forbidden, like in the days when I was a teenager and tried to keep something from my mom. Now it's my fourteen-year-old daughter!

My first question for fate: Why does he have to write now that Amir and I are trying to work things out? But his e-mail wasn't what I had expected; he only wrote that he had been glad to meet me and we should get together—*blah, blah, blah.* In a way, I'm relieved and somewhat disappointed. But, hey, everything happens for a reason, right? I'm not going to answer him yet.

Other that that there was nothing new. Amir and I talked a lot after dinner. It was like it used to be, except on a much more mature level. We're trying to take baby steps in the right direction. The problem is that this time we aren't blind and both of us have certain expectations.

I saw a movie a couple of years ago before this whole thing happened—I think it was called *The Story of Us* with Bruce Willis, who still looks so hot ☺—well, anyway, it was about a couple, and they wanted to get a divorce. At the end, the woman, played by Michelle Pfeiffer, said to him that they shouldn't end everything so quickly. She says that a marriage is like a city, which you build up slowly, and just because there are a couple of small earthquakes, you shouldn't throw out everything. That sentence stays in my mind. But my problem is that I'm not sure whether our fallouts are just small earthquakes or the beginning of a huge one.

Fifteen years ago, I was young and had no idea what I was doing. Now I'm much older, and I know what can go wrong, which makes it scarier for me. When I was telling my parents that Amir and I had decided to stay together, they were very excited for me. But I told my mom about my fear. She says it's natural and that I should, despite the past, concentrate only on the future. She should know because she has been married for forty-five years now.

See but the problem is that my mother's generation is different from mine. They were the ones who fought for women's rights and the ones who didn't, under any circumstances, want to be like their mother's generation. They taught us to be independent and use the freedom they had won, but they also forgot to tell us how to use it. All they taught us was you shouldn't be only a homemaker and mother; you have to use your talents. And, yes, I appreciate that. But tell me the best way to balance nurturing a happy marriage, being a good mother, and climbing the corporate ladder at the same time? Isn't it our society that thrusts us into these different roles and then discards us when we let one slip and don't meet expectations? I mean, come on, we know men who work their ass off *for* their family but are never home, and everyone praises them for it. And those same people treat us like traitors for having interests outside of the home. Right! It's so unfair.

When I was nineteen, I always thought I knew what I wanted from life. But here I am—married, separated, and married again. I have no idea what I am doing. I guess I should be happy now, but after the initial excitement of two days ago, I have started to re-evaluate and reality is sinking in. Maybe I gave in too quickly. Maybe I should have explained to him my conditions first. It's a good thing that I'm still keeping my distance.

I guess time will tell if I made the right decision. Okay, I have to get some sleep now.

January 14, 2006

I wish I could have slept in a little longer, but I had to get up at 7:30 AM to take Yasmin to her ice hockey game. I have no idea who made that pathetic schedule. Don't they know that people work and would love to enjoy a little bit of sleeping on Saturday morning? Yasmin loves hockey though; otherwise, I would have convinced her to stop. She's also getting really good at it. She's not constantly falling. They have a very good team, too, I should say. Just too bad that we could not go to the city, as the girls had suggested the other night.

The bleachers were, as usual, crowded with all these people, who think it's a little café for a breakfast of coffee and bagels. I kind of get it. But what I don't understand is why they drag the whole family out of bed just to watch one of their kids sliding around on the ice? Hello? It's not the final game of the season; it's just practice. Your two-year-old son doesn't really care how his brother is hitting on his line. I think I even saw one of the kids grow up at the practices there. I remember when he was a freshly born blondish boy. He probably took his first steps at the ice rink! Too funny. His first word was probably "ice," instead of "Mommy." Whatever!

I dragged myself through the whole day in such a tired stage that I was enjoying making fun of people. It's so hypocritical: Parents always tell their kids to mind their own business, and here I am writing in my diary and complaining about everyone else. I'm just so happy no one can read this. I guess Lili and Yasmin would freak out over the "childish" ways of their oh-so-grown-up mother.

In the afternoon, we took the girls to the movies. It was great. I'm always too lazy and probably too stingy to go to the movie theater, but every time I get there, I think that I should probably go more often, But honestly, who can afford fifteen bucks per ticket? For one person it's fine, but for every week for a whole family plus drinks and popcorn, that's around one hundred bucks times four weeks. Oy!

January 15, 2006

Tonight Amir tried to seduce me. I guess the strap of my new bra was showing under my sweater and that must have turned him on. He said he had forgotten how beautiful I was. I just had to laugh like a bashful teenager. (Men really will do anything to get it.) I appreciated his compliment, but I still need time. I don't want to melt again. And I know that this is exactly what would happen.

I read somewhere—I think it was one of those women magazines in the doctor's waiting room—that men usually feel very weak before getting sex so much so that they behave like little boys begging for it and women get like that after the sex. So it's only natural that the woman is in control for as long as possible. That way we still can hold the strings to our men in our hands and treat them as puppets because we are still in control and, at that point, they will do anything.

So why not take advantage?

I guess because we care about the emotional side of intimacy, that's why we don't get an orgasm as quickly and most of us have to fake it. Something in me still loves Amir so much that I can feel my heart explode, but I'm so scared of giving in and being disappointed once again. Maybe it's just me.

Jessica once told me that she would have the worst fights with her boyfriend, but if he came forward right after it, she would immediately want to take off her clothes. I asked her how she could do it with someone who had just yelled at her. She said that she looked at it as pure sexual satisfaction with no emotional strings attached. I told her I wasn't sure if I could do that. I guess I'm more old-fashioned than I want to admit; I still believe in romantic lovemaking and don't see the act as the same as rat-fucking.

I don't know; I guess I see the difference in how people get together. But take out the mechanics of the act itself, and there's a huge difference between sex and lovemaking. For sex, you just want to satisfy yourself; you don't necessarily care about with whom. You like them just for that moment. In lovemaking, your priority is to make your partner happy before you think about your own needs and wants. No one ever says that a man who does it with prostitutes makes love to them. He pays her to have his own fun. I've never heard that a customer asked a whore whether she enjoyed it.

So maybe I'm right in my assumption and Jessica is wrong. But if it works for her, so what?

Okay, my hand hurts now from my little freedom speech on analyzing sex.

Tomorrow we'll be going to Amy's house for dinner. I'll tell you how it goes, since Amir hates Amy, from the first moment I introduced her as my oldest and dearest friend. These two manage to get into a huge discussion about the most stupid topics when they see each other. First, they start jokingly, but then the joke disappears and all you hear is personal attacking.

January 16, 2006

Work was work: same old people and same bitchy boss. I had to leave exactly at 5:00 PM but was scrutinized by this stupid guy at my office named James. I don't even know what exactly he is hired for. He is not a graphic artist, he doesn't do Marketing or Finance. Once I actually asked him if he was the doorman and lost his way to the offices. Needless to say that I didn't win a friend with my comment. He watched me packing up at me at 4:58 PM and gave me the nastiest look. Then he actually came up to me and asked me why I was leaving because during the last staff meeting we had been told that our arrival and departure time had to be on the hour. I shot back a nasty look and asked him if, as a designer, my creative time also had to be programmed to his clock. James raised his voice, just to make sure that the director of the department—I honestly don't even know his name! That's how important he is to me!—would hear him and remember him for the next promotion. I was shaking with anger—still am—as he said that I had to wait two more minutes and then get ready to leave. I looked back and just said, because he had been talking so much, the time had already passed!

That stupid boy pretended he was my boss. I can't believe this. I went and studied so hard in order to have fun at my job and not drag myself into an office where I would feel like a wingless bird every morning, and now this freshly graduated child is telling me what I should do! I'm ready to tell him that he should change his diapers first!

Because of this long ordeal, I had to drive like a maniac to get home, quickly fix something for dinner, and then immediately drive Lili to her ballet rehearsal. Because it was only a one-hour practice, it would have been ridiculous to drive back, so I had to wait with a very unhappy Yasmin, who had to finish her homework by sitting on the floor and using the bench as a desk.

We got home at 7:30 PM, and by the time the girls were finished with homework and ready for bed, it was close to 9:30 PM. Amir came home and complained about both girls being awake and telling me that I should be stricter. I nearly exploded. I was able to control myself though. After all, didn't we just agree to try again? Well, I don't want to be the reason why it won't work. I just told him the whole schedule, but what really pissed me off was when he said, "Well, don't take them to all these classes!" I mean, come on! Isn't he the one who gave our kids his last name? Isn't he the one who is called the head of the family? Isn't he the one who sits in the audience during their performances and enjoys the show? Isn't he the one who shows everyone the pictures of *his* kids and very quickly collects the compliments? Without lifting a finger. That really makes me mad.

You know I work and earn some money, so that is seen by everyone, but the work I do as a mother is never seen. Sometimes I think that he forgets that it takes time, energy, persistence, and discipline, next to the obvious motherly love, to raise two kids. It's unrealistic that humans are babies and then—poof!—they are adults. But some men, like Amir, forget all the unpaid work behind the success.

It's like someone who goes into a shop and buys a shirt. Now he has a tangible asset, which can be seen and touched and is a reminder of the whole contract. But imagine hiring a contractor, using his services, but saying that you can't see the hard work behind the success. Everything done by a mother, or maybe in some cases the father, is seen as a parental duty.

But my question is, who sets the standard? If it's the mother in the rich Western society, then the Sudanese mother who isn't able to rescue her child from the lions or in the beginning of the 1980s from the enemy attacks isn't taking care of her children. If the Sudanese mother is setting the standard, then the mother in the West isn't taking care of her children because she might bring them to daycare so she can go to work. This way of thinking is all too one-sided to me. I think every mother has to know, depending on her own circumstances, what she can afford—not just financially, but also timewise.

I know I sometimes judge those super-career moms as well, for bringing their children to daycare and not even being there when the kids get sick. I actually knew one, who booked her vacation the exact week of her daughter's twelfth birthday! And, of course, I gossiped about it, but now when I think about it, I realize that I barely knew anything about her. Maybe she had had her reasons to do what she was doing, or maybe again she just had had her kids as prestige kids. I don't know, but I think even I'm too quick to judge people.

I guess you'll see the results only when the kids grow up. I always like to think that I should be good to my kids based on my own personal standards because in the end they will decide which nursing home I end up in. And if I really succeed they'll visit me more than once every other week.

January 17, 2006

I think I ended up with Yasmin's strep throat. I feel so sick with a headache, stomachache, and scratchy throat. Well, my mommy didn't take me to the doctor and get my medication. ☹ I still had to get up and prepare the girls' breakfast, drive them to school, and go to work. I would have loved to call in sick, but then I wouldn't have had any sick days left in case the girls got sick or there were school snow days. That's another unfair thing in my house! If there were snow days or school cancellations for whatever reason, Amir would never think to take a day off. It has to be me. Sure, I love to spend time with Lili and Yasmin, but how am I ever supposed to get a promotion if I'm never there? Well, maybe *never* is a little exaggerated, but if this continues, no one will be able to count on me.

When I was hired, they originally told me that on those days when my kids took me out of the office I could log on from home, so that I could have access to my client files. Because most of my work is drawing, I thought I could do my job anywhere my heart desired. Yeah, right! Now they freak out if you just leave your seat to go to the bathroom! And the economy isn't even that bad. Maybe I should try to switch departments within the company. I have other skills, which are useful. But then again, Liz would need to sign off on that, and I'm sure she wouldn't.

The more I think about it, the more I like the idea of getting my PhD and going into academia. This way I could be my own boss, and I would have the summers off and join the girls when they go to visit my parents in France. That sounds like a very good idea. I'll consult with my mom tomorrow and get her advice. Maybe she'll also have an idea about how to finance it. I won't tell Amir anything yet; he always freaks out when there is change.

I once read a book about organizational behavior. I still remember the chart in it. I guess it's called Lewis method of change or something like that. There are these three different stages every person go through during change. Accepting the change, adapting to a new situation, and then freezing with the new habits.

I always like change, which is exactly the opposite of Amir, who would just love for everything to stay the same. I guess ever since we started talking about our relationship, I've started analyzing everything! I guess I should get a PhD in psychology! Ha ha! Imagine me as a shrink! Well, anyway, regardless of all this, I truly have to find a solution for my present situation.

January 19, 2006

I *hate* my work! Seriously! I became a designer to be creative and somehow change the world, but reality is that I constantly have to run from meeting to meeting to basically sell my artistry. I would love to smash a phone on Liz's head while screaming if I wanted to be a saleswoman, I would have become a saleswoman! But what's the use. If I quit, I sit at home and do what?

I imagine the first couple of weeks would be fun—reading some books, going out with friends, and doing everything I can't do now, but then what? Well, I started looking into the different job-hunting Web sites. Maybe I've been here way too long, and it's time for a change. If I asked Amir, he would want things to always stay the same. I can't live like that; I need new stimuli. But the job market and job-hunting methods have changed so much from the last time I looked. Everything is online now, and there's so much out there. It makes me so confused that I don't even know where to start. I updated my résumé and posted it on two of the Web sites, so we'll see what happens.

I have to get out of here; otherwise I'll literally die.

January 20, 2006

One of the places called me this morning, and they would like me to come in on Monday for an interview. I'm so excited.

When I picked Lili up from school, she was telling me so many new things about the kids at school. I guess all these kiddies must have had some hormonal rollercoaster shift over the holidays. Seriously, I think around Christmas season they all change—for the good or bad. Anyway, Lili and Jen are very close friends. Because of that people make up the stupidest stories. Today one of their so-called friends, Rose, started screaming at them that their friendship was almost like a marriage and that Lili and Jen had some issues. I mean, for heaven's sake, you girls are fourteen! Get a life! What's wrong with two girls not being bitchy to each other? Is it a problem to be normal friends? I told Lili to ignore it and continue her friendship to Jen. I tried to play it down in front of her, but internally I was fuming.

Jane, Rose's mom, called later that evening, which only will make matters worse. Thank goodness, Lili doesn't know. I can't believe that the moms do this at their age! I would rather die than call up a mom and tell her, "My daughter is really upset that your daughter is not inviting her over anymore...." What do they want, mommy–daughter play dates? It's one thing if it's bullying, which I would definitely get involved in, but complaining why two kids are friends?

Anyway, Jane started the conversation lightly and talked about the weather, work, etc. But I knew it was coming—and bang! She dropped the bomb. Her daughter likes Lili, but because Lili is always hanging out with Jen, her daughter and Lili are never able to spend time together—blah, blah, blah. She said that her daughter never said anything and that she never screamed, but she was the victim of this stuck-like-glue friendship. Why do some people pretend their kids are the answer to the world's prayers? Man, I hate these sudden phone confrontations. It's like chopping someone's head of.

I told her that I had no idea what she was talking about—which is wrong because now she will think that Lili never tells me anything about school—and I would talk to Lili in the morning. I also told her that the girls were big enough to handle these things themselves. She agreed but then went on and on, like a never-ending tape.

After we said good-bye and hung up, I thought that it was maybe my own fault of befriending a friend's mom. You know, there is always the mother's side of the story, which is what her own child has told her. By revealing it, she is defending her child based on half of the story and at the same time risking her friendship. I think that from now on I should keep more distance—a so-called respect level—from the mothers of Lili's and Yasmin's friends. That way I don't get to know the parents enough to know the family their brat is from. Then the kids are forced to handle their disagreements themselves, and only when it gets to really bad, would I get involved.

In this situation, I think no matter what happened Rose told Jane to call me, but what Jane doesn't know though is that I'm usually a very patient person and only snap at the last straw. Jane is just pretending everything is everyone else's fault and that her daughter is Mother Teresa. Hello? Wake up. Your daughter is the one spreading rumors?

Well, anyway, I'll tell Lili tomorrow morning in a calm way. Although it's good that she and Jen are so close, maybe there's a pinch of truth that they ignore others and you shouldn't burn bridges. You never know when you might see people again and need their help.

So enough about my philosophy on child psychology. I finally want to watch a movie tonight—with Amir.

January 21, 2006

I shouldn't have watched a movie and stayed up that late. I completely forgot that I had to get up at 7:00 AM and take Yasmin to hockey. I *still* wonder who sets up the schedule for the ice rink. Again, it's weekend, and people actually like to sleep in! But Yasmin likes it, so I'll continue taking her.

Guess who sent me an e-mail this morning? Ben. I had nearly forgotten about him. Seriously! He wrote that he was in New York again and that he was thinking about me. He wondered why I never wrote him back—oh, and he hopes that everything is going well. While I was waiting for Yasmin at the ice arena, I called him. I still have mixed feelings about the whole thing. Maybe the guy really wants to be involved in only business. But then on the other hand, I felt something, and to top it off, I was nervous dialing his number. I never get nervous when calling a business associate! Although I like the tickle and this makes everything more exciting, I don't want to play with fire. Sometimes I'm not sure about my relationship with Amir. Yes, I do love him, but then again, I'm not sure whether I'm in love with him now or the man he was fifteen years ago.

Last week I was talking to Anja, the girl from accounting, not about my own life but relationships in general. She has worked as a marriage counselor for years, so she should know all about that. She basically said things that you know but never think about—like that we evolve and a relationship requires a continuous work by both parties, compromise, and time alone. I know. But what do you do when there is a gap in time or when you decided a couple of times to end it all and then get back together again? Do you start from scratch, pretending that you just met this person you knew before? I don't think that's possible because there's so much that has already happened. You can forgive one another but never forget. There have been just too many things that have been said and done. I know some people who literally start from scratch. But I'm not sure that I can forget and pretend all those years of cold war between Amir and me never existed.

I do miss him, but I guess I miss the man in my fantasy who looks just like Amir. It's this picture of him I have in my mind. I'm very scared that one of us will get too stressed and explode again, and then that picture will disintegrate in the inferno.

Plus, I don't want to ever separate from him on bad terms. He'll always be the father of my children and the man I truly passionately loved at one point in my life. But I'm scared of looking at him one day and thinking, *Who is this?* Again, another one of the issues I have with marriage: It makes you take the other person for granted! Maybe if Amir and I had lived separately geographically, we would have missed the times we had and each other in a different way, It would have made us appreciate what we had. Or maybe neither of us was ready to commit fully when we got married.

I know, after fifteen years and two beautiful kids, it's pathetic to think about all of this. What bothers me a lot is that we constantly separate and get back together. As I listen to my friends, I know that none of them has a perfect relationship—not that that exists to begin with.—but from what I know, none of them ever separated and reunited. It was either a clean cut or a final commitment. That's what drives me insane: I feel like a line broken between two pages, hesitant and uninformed about my status. I'm legally married, but sometimes I'm not in a relationship. Does that even make sense?

January 22, 2006

Today was Amir's birthday! The girls had prepared him some homemade gifts, and I got him a shirt and a book that he had mentioned once. We made him a cake and prepared a very nice dinner. See, that's where we really get along; we can have a good time on the birthdays with good yummy dinners and "real" thoughtful gifts—you know, not just buying something to buy something.

Well, tonight it happened. After such a long time, we made love. I was very shy; I felt like a teenage virgin again. I can't even describe it; I felt different and more mature, but also I longed for more. Before him I had only been with one man, so when I met him, he, as the experienced one, was more the boss and I was the little girl. Even though I haven't had more experience, he made me feel like a woman this time. Maybe it's also the way I see myself, my body, and my desires. As a grown-up woman, I expect different things and am not willing to compromise on certain things.

Now, afterward, I'm not even sure it was a good idea. I also think that he was very irritated. He didn't say anything, but I felt his confusion at how things had changed. I know I'm becoming a pessimist, but after such heartbreak, I'm really scared to give in too quickly and be disappointed again. And I'm also not sure how he'll evaluate my new sexual awakening. I guess we'll see.

January 23, 2006

What a day! I had sent out my résumé to a company. It was nothing serious, just to see how much I was worth on the job market. They called me back, and there I was on my way to the interview. I decided to take the train into the city because of the snow. I thought it would be way more relaxing.

Ha ha! Well, I'm laughing about it now, but this morning I was ready to cry.

I parked my car at the train station and got my ticket (I never realized the ticket booth ladies—you know the usually large women, who my mom would tell me was born and grew up in the booth—had disappeared). Everything was going fine until I caught my shoe in an ice block, actually a hole in the pavement with ice over it, and my heel broke! Yes, it was my nice Pradas that I reserve for interviews.

Now, what do I do without a heel?

I walked back, extracted it from the hole, and went from door to door asking for glue. People must have thought I was insane. But again, this is New York we're talking about where anything is possible. I guess I have lived in the suburbs for too long.

Finally, I found a *Duane Read* store who had some crazy glue, and just to be safe, I taped the heel to the rest of the shoe as well. I'm so glad that it was winter and I was wearing a pantsuit, so that no one could see the shoe. Those kinds of things always happen to me.

The interview itself was okay. The woman who had called me was very nice but the other one there—oh man, so much ego in one person! She had no sense of humor and didn't even smile when she entered the room. I think she didn't even care about my résumé. She just decided from her first glance that she didn't like me. Well, but I'm not going to get discouraged. That was the first, but definitely not the last interview I'll have. We'll see what happens. The nice woman said that they would have a decision by the end of the week, and she would call me. It's a good thing that I'm not desperate but just looking around to see what's out there.

When I told Amir, he laughed about the heel story, and the girls thought it was hilarious. After the girls went to bed, Amir told me I was scatterbrained and unfocused because I was looking for a job. I tried to explain to him that I needed to keep my options open, but it just wouldn't go into his head. He said that I have utopian ideas when it came to work and I was waiting for the perfect job. But that's not true. I know that on some days any job can get on your nerves, but hey, he must be happy; otherwise he wouldn't have survived at his job for the past ten years, right? He just doesn't understand.

January 24, 2006

I knew something would go wrong! Today his mother called and started in on me. Oh my gosh! She explained that she feels so lonely, misses her son, and all that nonsense—blah, blah, blah! It's like some women still perfume their houses with their son's pee! Maybe that's why some Middle Eastern men—or men in general—are the way they are! It just kills me that they want a second mommy who is their cook *and* their whore!

What is this? I mean really *what is this?*

Amir's mom asks me constantly whether I take care of her son! I mean, hello, I should be responsible for my girls and not for wrapping your son's penis in blue silk, right? Did I get a lifetime companion or a forty-year-old baby? What bothers me the most is that the women of her generation are the ones who tried to escape from these imposed boundaries on females. Were they not the ones who burned the bras just to show the liberation of women? Why is she now behaving as if that never happened? Tell me!

This entire double standard just makes me sick. After all, it was okay for her to take another woman's son and behave like a total bitch toward his family. And she was and still is Mrs. Holy Saint!

She must have heard from someone that I was job hunting again, and of course that might have given her the idea that her beloved son is starving in the kitchen and the bedroom. I would love tell her that I still cook—just because of my girls—and sexually his appetite was never huge—at least not when it came to me.

You know, I have these weird ideas sometimes. I've accused him of cheating already even though I'm not sure whether that's the right word for our relationship. Why else would a man not show interest for the woman he is with? There are these stupid, or maybe not-so-stupid tests on different Web sites, called something like "Is he cheating on you?" I was reading one and thought that Amir would be the best sample. But on the other hand, he's just not the type to take them. I always thought his whole testosterone level was messed up. Once, were not not even separated at that time, he told me once that he couldn't make love to a woman. It had to be a whore he fucks. Great! How can I save this relationship? Dress in a leather mini with thigh boots and a black lace bra with condoms attached to a belt, stand at the door as he comes home, and ask him if he's interested in giving me a ride? I mean, let's put the whole incident from two nights ago aside. I'll look at it as something special and not generalize about one night

January 25, 2006

Yesterday's phone call with Amir's mom is still on my mind. I keep thinking as I replay it, *What makes a man?* It's not as easy to answer as you might think.

Zorba would have said, "What's in his heart and what's in his pants."

In ancient times they would have said, "A man is one who defends his country."

In the caveman times, he would have been the person who hunted and brought home the food.

Then for a time a man wasn't considered a man unless he had produced a son.

Okay, I get the different definitions. They all depend on what society wanted at the time and mostly what the expectations were for the male species. But now, after I have been called a wisecracking, man-castrating woman, I really want to know: What makes a man? Is it just his biological equipment? I swear I've not chopped off anyone's male body parts—yet. So in my estimation that doesn't make them men.

Is it the money part, the fact that they bring home the financial security? No, this can't be either, since after World War II women have been able to work in factories. That's when the underground women's movement started until women burned their bras at the beginning of the 1970s and publicly declared their freedom. The rest is history. We women can—in most countries—do whatever our hearts desire.

So just because I'm fine opening my own car door or can paint a room *and* the ceiling without a man's help castrates men? Or is it the fact that I can think on my own, say what I think, and not let anyone, regardless of gender, tell me what to think? Maybe it's that I like to be treated like a woman but accepted as a woman. Those are two completely different things, which men still don't get.

I honestly believe men didn't evolve with the women's movement even though they had more than a generation to get used to it. Come on, guys, the fact that we women decide about our bodies, our brains, and our money doesn't mean we don't accept or respect you, so why is it so difficult for you to see the different roles we have in society? Is it the fact that women can occupy several roles at once? Does the fact that I work eight hours a day; come home and prepare dinner; drive my kids to after-school activities; watch over their homework; take care of the house by cleaning, doing laundry, and shopping; and talk to my children make me a castrator of men? Maybe I'm expecting too much from men. Maybe they just didn't get used to multitasking women. Then again, they were probably too busy thinking about their manhood, and we all know that men can't multitask.

January 26, 2006

I truly want to send my two kids to a third-world country for a while. Why is it that they take everything they have for granted? Maybe I spoil them too much, but then what mother doesn't want the best for her kids? I think that I might have gone overboard though. All the unhappiness in my marriage was turned into affection for my kids. Now all I hear is, "I want this; I want that…" I just don't want to hear it anymore.

What happened to kids who had to earn their luxuries? I don't necessarily mean with money, but how about do this, before you get that. You know clean your room if you want to go to the movies with your friends. No one asks me, "What do you think about this? Do you like paying for this?" Sometimes I blame myself. I think those moms who don't—well, I don't want to say love or care—go overboard for their kids are appreciated more. The smallest thing they do gets immediate attention because there are no expectations.

But, no, everything is taken for granted. I have to work, I have to cook, and I have to shop. Oh yes, and heaven forbid if I complain in public. Then Amir and his family stamp me as a terrible mother and who knows what else. I'm sick and tired of this. Why don't people understand that I love being a mom, but yes, I have a life, a name, and some free time for myself as well? I didn't start existing after becoming a mother, right? So why do I feel like a slave?

Amir tells me that as an emancipated woman it's my duty to pay for half of the kids' expenses. Meanwhile I feel they want everything on planet Earth and won't take no for an answer. And I'm simply tired of fighting on both fronts. Why is it that no matter what a mother decides turns out to be the wrong choice? I wish in addition to all the classes I have had in my life, I would have taken a class on raising of teenage kids. Now that's a good idea. Maybe I should start one. Here's a sample syllabus:

Lesson 1: Just be prepared for extreme hormonal rollercoasters.

Lesson 2: Pack your stuff, run, and be prepared to come back after they finish college.

January 28, 2006

Okay, if I tell you what I heard today in the office, you'll probably wonder what I would hear if I even sought out the gossip. Two of the girls were standing behind me and going, "No—really!" the whole time. I was ready to turn around and scream at them, "Shut the fuck up! I have a deadline!" But then something caught my attention, and I just pretended to work because the deadline could wait for five minutes. Liz had heard that Holly from marketing had had an affair with Bill from finance. I thought, *Holly? That shy invisible girl had an affair with a married man? Sure, Bill is a good catch—but he isn't a catch when he wears the certain piece of jewelry?*

Then I wondered, *What makes a woman start an affair with a married man? What kind of woman and what kind of man is necessary?* I always used to bash the one who was married and too weak to break up with one person before starting something with another. I still believe that—but with some amendments. I guess you have to look at the entire situation. What makes a man's eye wander? Bill has a good financial situation, has a beautiful wife who works as a corporate attorney in a famous law firm, and is simply a dream woman come true. Why would he look to Holly? She is truly average—not very bright, average body, okay looks—no man would go after her ass. What makes her so confident to be a home wrecker?

Based on Liz's story it all started during last year's Christmas party. Yes, those holidays can be a time when people get too friendly to their coworkers—but back to my main story. Holly obviously saw an opportunity in Bill. Bill—what did he see in her as a mistress? Her youth? Again, if she had been a leggy lingerie model or looked like

Miss Corporate World, I would have said, "Yes." I thought of Bills' wife—I forgot her name because she is mostly on business trips or in meetings and never attends any of the company functions. "She works like a maniac"—that's what he says.

Oh, and then it hit me. Bill was looking for a woman. It didn't matter to him who she was; he was looking for something he didn't have at home. He had the successful, beautiful lady at home, so he had to look for her opposite. If he had had an average woman at home, he would have been looking for the sexy one. So basically, he had the I Want Something Different syndrome.

She, on the other hand, became a rich man's mistress even though she knows that he's never going to leave his wife. Why? I mean, sure, she might not get a man like Bill to marry her, but she was able to become his mistress. Man, she must be good in bed to keep him for so long, considering that most men would use her for only a one-night fuck. Once I heard her say that she never intended to get married. At that time, I just thought, *What an obnoxious girl! She's too full of herself. What makes her think that she is better by not stepping into the misery?* I guess she was smarter.

And then it hit me. I put two and two together. Women become married men's mistresses because they don't want to play wife. Don't laugh; I know it sounds so simple. But think about it. What does a wife get? Sure, she gets half in a divorce. But she also gets all the complaints about increasing mortgage interest rates; she gets the complaints about the yard work on the weekend; she gets the whole "I'm not in the mood for your family and friends" attitude. The wife also gets the "I have so much work; I have meetings and business trips" excuse. And the mistress? What does she get? A man who comes to her for a good time of lovemaking, champagne by the fireplace, and diamond necklaces to make her shut up. Pretty good deal, huh?

I wouldn't do it though, regardless of the good time, how horrible the wife might be, how great the guy is. Sorry, a guy who doesn't break off his marriage first can't be great.

But then again, I guess it all depends on our culture and how we were raised. Sometimes—well, a lot of times actually—I envy the French. Remember how they reacted when they found out that their president had had an affair? *"Monsieur le Président comprend l'amour."* Man, the guy had his wife, his kids, his mistress, and his love child at his funeral. That is one woman too much! Sometimes I think that people like that are much happier in their life. I mean, it's like having one woman or one man for each occasion. It's not like I have one shirt in my closet that I can wear to shop, work, and waltz! So why not have a man for every occasion and then one to manage them all? Ha! That would be fun. But it's maybe too dreamy. I would probably be the first to fire all of them—too much testosterone, you know.

Now I just wonder what will happen between Bill and his wife and Bill and Holly. See, I don't need a television in my house because I have too much drama here at work anyway. Who needs a soap opera? Will tell you more when I find out. Stay tuned as the shows used to say before commercial breaks.

January 29, 2006

I truly wonder who said that every child should have at least four after-school activities. I think whoever it was wanted to make parents work really hard and not have a weekend. It would be great if I could see my kids on Saturdays not at a rink, in a ballet studio, or on a soccer field. Maybe my kids are losing their interest in activities because they seem to be too busy complaining about getting up on Saturdays. I try not to show them that the feeling is mutual. And although it's true, nothing makes me prouder than seeing them succeed after all their hard work. I look at them, when they aren't watching me, and think, *Hey, that's my baby! Look at her!*

I know how they would react if they knew how I felt about it. Both would roll their eyes simultaneously and say, "Oh, here she goes again!" I guess it takes a mom to understand it. As a young girl, I never wanted to have children of my own. Selfishness, stretch marks, fallings boobs, weight gain, sleepless nights, and responsibility all what came with a baby, and I wasn't interested in any of that.

I remember both of the times I went to the doctor's office and found out that I was expecting. Each one was different, but the feeling of someone is pouring hot water over my head was the same. With Lili I thought, *I'll never be able to be a good mom. I just know it; I can't possibly take care of this small creature.* My biggest concern was that she might slip out of my hand when I was trying to bathe her. Now when I think about it, it brings tears to my eyes and a smile to my face. With Yasmin, it was different I guess. I had joy that Lili would have a companion, but my concern wasn't that I was incapable; it was how I could balance it all.

How would I split myself between the two kids? Even with one child, a mom doesn't have enough time to herself, but add another one? How would I change diapers for both, prepare bottles of milk, and bathe them?

I remember the first time I bathed them at the same time. It was such an accomplishment that I called nearly everyone I knew and told them about it. Now as I look back, I remember being so exhausted after that two-hour bath.

When I see my children growing up in front of me, I get these flashbacks. And because all of the baby stuff is done, I have more time to hone my maternal instincts as I watch them. Now I find myself wanting to hold them and hug them more than when they were little. Back then they needed me physically to feed or change them. Don't get me wrong— they still need me, but it's different. Now they want to make sure that I'm watching their back..

I think being a mom is the most demanding and challenging, yet most beautiful and satisfying—hmm, I don't want to call it a job—career of a woman's life.

January 30, 2006

Believe it or not, I had never heard of the term *PMS* before I moved to this country. It might be because I don't "suffer" from this syndrome; neither does anyone I know or maybe it's just that no one ever talked about it. (When I heard of the term at some point I mixed it up with PMI, which is a pre-mortgage insurance!) Now it seems like *every* woman I know talks at least once a month about PMSing.

As mentioned, I don't have this syndrome, but I think most of the *men* I know do! Recently I was sitting with my former college girls, Cindy and Diane in a café and we realized it. No, it's not a cultural or age thing because my husband is Iranian, Cindy's is South Korean, and Diane's is American, and they are all different ages and have different jobs. The only common denominator is: *gender*. Okay, I know from statistics that a sample group needs at least thirty pieces of data, but we'll cheat a little and use only these three.

And yes, they all have PMS and actually it's not monthly but daily. Every day Amir finds something that went wrong. He craves certain food, it is too loud in the house, he gets irritated easily. One day he is so constipated, the other he is bloating, then his back hurts, he has difficulty falling asleep, his head hurts, oh my... the list could go on and one. Next thing he probably asks me to get him some tampons!

I told the girls how my grandmother always used to say, "Be patient with men." But you know what? I think since we women started emancipating ourselves, we stopped being patient. For all these years, I always left him alone when he comes home, didn't complain about things, and tried to be a little like a housewife of the 1950s. Cindy and Diane almost fell from their chairs they were laughing. Yes, picturing me as a traditional housewife is very funny! But you know, within the past year, my patience has been hanging on by a very thin thread. I wish Amir didn't know that I don't get PMS and that he would treat me with the same patience I have treated him with daily for the past fifteen years.

My personal advice to men: Be patient, smile, and act like a man from the new millennium.

January 31, 2006

Today our department was called into Liz's office—and guess what? We're all laid off.

She told us, "The economy isn't doing well, and we really appreciate our good work, but—"

I kept thinking they should say it aloud that we were being laid off and stop giving us this ass-kissing nonsense. Do they think it really works to send someone for a hair cut before putting them under the guillotine? Of course not, so why don't companies learn? Just drop the fucking bomb! The VPs and the big shots don't give a damn, so why does HR have to be so pathetically stupid?

Liz also told us, "Your client doesn't want to continue with further projects but we will definitely keep your résumé on file." And that was it. Done. Finished. Over. So over.

I've no idea why I'm even upset or sad since I wanted to quit anyway. But the fact that they even ruined my good-bye bothers me. It really sucks. I had visualized how I would get another job first and then walk in to the bitch lady's office and say, "And good-bye!" Well, I cleaned out my desk and packed up, and that was it. But at least they are paying us two weeks' salary. As is standard in the industry, I guess they didn't want to see the miserable faces around them, knowing that everyone would take client names and confidential material before leaving.

When I got home and told the girls, they didn't know whether to be happy that I could take them to school in the morning and have a good dinner ready when they got home or be sad that I had just lost my disposable income. I guess we all will have to get used to this new situation. I just wish I had heard about last week's interview.

People usually say that you should always be networking. Okay, so I guess I should start with that, but you can't walk around and write on your forehead "Hey those with jobs available, I'm looking for one, so get me one *now*." Some people don't understand that networking takes a lot of time and can't be done every day. I guess I'll have to dig out old address books and contacts, give them a call, start the conversations talking about the weather again, and hope something sticks. And I have to deal with the unemployment office, which is a complete nightmare.

Amir makes good money, but what bothers me is that he doesn't know that I need to have a job for my sanity. I have to go out in the morning and see people. I have to feel as if my work is worth something, which includes financial value. He just doesn't get it. His reaction was something like, "Oh, I'm so sorry. Well, good thing we're still living in one house, so you don't have to worry about the mortgage." I mean come on! There's more to it. I'll lose my mind if I'm unemployed. What am I supposed to do at home? Clean the basement and look at my nails? I don't want to sit home.

But I don't even know what I want in a job. Obviously, I wasn't happy with what I had before.

The bad luck is just soaking into my life. Some people have a bad relationship and a good career. Some people have a healthy relationship and a bad career. But why do I have to get the bad side of both? I'm just so fucking tired of this. I just want to crawl into my bed right now and sleep, but I have to figure out something.

February 1, 2006

Okay, so this was my first day sitting at home. It was good to make all the beds for a change. I ended up doing the oh-so-necessary laundry in the laundry room, which already looked like Mount Everest. I put the clothes away into the girl's closets and made a fabulous dinner. It was a real lunch, not grab-and-go sandwiches. Both girls were delighted, and I just enjoyed seeing their excitement.

"It's so funny, Mom, that you're starting to act like a mother," Yasmin said. Then I brought out a dessert, and she got so excited that she said, "Wow, you made this, too?"

I guess it's true when they say that children need a mom who cares about them. Maybe it was good that the entire layoff thing happened, so that I could see my girls get excited over a bowl of *mousse au chocolat*. I was able to sit down with them, set the table, and look at their faces while they ate. It felt great.

I even got the chance to ask them about their homework and help them with some of it. They were delighted.

I guess this was a really good day.

February 2, 2006

I have no words to write. Still remember Mary? She used to live next door and then she and her husband built a house and hence moved away. Beautiful property, I was invited to her home-warming. Well, anyway, she left a message, saying that her husband has cancer. The man is forty years old! He has two little kids and a wife. I'm speechless. I called back, and she said I should come by. On my way to the grocery store, I stopped at their home, which is the most welcoming place on earth. I mean you literally feel all the love they have in the décor of this place they call home. They had just bought the house and renovated it. I saw Mike, and he tried to smile and play the entire thing down, but I could see that he's so nervous. Apparently, he had been complaining for a while about vision and hearing problems and went to the doctor to get better glasses. Well, it turns out he has a brain tumor, which is growing. Don't ask me about all the medical terms, but they have to make a decision whether to have a surgery or send him to radiation.

When Mary left the room for ten minutes to check on their kids, Mike told me how scared he was—not for himself, but more for Mary and the kids. He said that he had read and heard about the treatment, but experiencing it on your own is a completely different story. He said that no one, unless they had been there, could ever understand how it felt when the doctor came into the office with a straight face and told him, "You have cancer." He didn't know whether he should tell the doc that he didn't believe it or start crying. *How do I come home to tell Mary?* he said he asked himself as the doctor went over his options. He mentioned that when he left the doc's office in a trance, he looked at everyone on the street. As he drove home, he looked at the people in their cars. He started to smell the air and look at the details in everything that he saw. For the first time, he noted the pattern on streetlights. I told him that I had never noticed that. He said that probably not many people pay attention to these things until they find out that their ability to notice them might come to an end soon.

He's right. We all rush through our lives and run from one thing to the next, constantly focused on the big picture. I'm just as guilty. But isn't it true that sometimes the small points make the entire picture? Shouldn't we sometimes stop, smell the flowers, and smile at someone in order to make their day?

The good part is that they're financially secure and have a good insurance. But regardless, Mike was worried about how Mary would handle the stress. Here's a man who dearly loves his family, and his first thought is how his wife will take it after he has been diagnosed with this fatal disease. He said that ever since he broke the news this morning, he has taken sixty seconds to enjoy every detail of her face. Sixty seconds?

"That's not a lot," I replied.

He smiled and nodded. "No, it's not a lot of time for someone who is rushing, but it can be a lifetime if you enjoy every single second of it."

Wow, I thought. *What a big statement. It's so true.*

He said that ever since he has known that he might not always be around, he really wants to utilize his senses. He told me that they had dinner last night, and he noticed that the potatoes were so soft that they melted with the butter. He took in the taste of his wine and the texture of the table; he smelled the flowers and realized that he liked the fact that Mary always had candles burning. It had taken his getting cancer to notice all these things, he noted as he laughed sadly.

I was in deep thought on my way home. His sentences were tattooed on my brain: *Sixty seconds can be a lifetime if you enjoy every single second of it.*

February 17, 2006

There's still nothing on the job front. I'm getting more and more frustrated by the minute. I have had one phone interview so far, and I can see on job boards that recruiters are looking at my résumé which impresses me already. I always thought those job boards and search engines were just a fancy Internet presence for companies.

One of the recruiters told me that it usually takes around three months to find a new job. We'll see. After this last phone interview, I think it will most likely take me three years to find something. It's unbelievable how interviewing is actually an art. This guy on the phone was asking such weird questions that he got me completely confused. Then he got confused, and at the end I had no idea whether I had called a local restaurant to order pizza or actually wanted to be hired for a job.

It was worse than the January interview, which cost me a shoe.

I remember in the past we didn't have phone interviews. It's so different when you're trying to judge by someone's voice what he or she actually wants from you. That's why I was ready to yell at this guy. He made no sense at all. He asked me a little about my résumé, then about this and that, and then checked the job posting to see whether I was even applying for a job at his company. I guess he didn't even know that he had posted a job after all.

My point is that maybe they shouldn't constantly advertise about how people should brush up their résumés, write the perfect cover letter, and make the perfect impression in an interview. Instead why not offer a class and teach people how to interview properly? Hello? I mean police officers and lawyers have to learn how to ask strategic questions that build a case and have a point. Why not recruiters? Maybe they do have a class, but it seems as if it just isn't working.

At the end, I was so tired of answering "Excuse me?", "Pardon me?", "Yes, yes, I've done this", or "No, no, I haven't done that", that I was relieved to hang up.

I guess I'll just scrub toilets at the train stations—unless I need to interview, of course.

March 1, 2006

I had dinner with a couple of the girls. Of course, Laura had to bring up the problem of marriages, and we ended moving topics from the office and politics, to kitchen chitchat, and then bedroom talk. They knew that Amir and I don't sleep in the same room any longer. Anna said that her husband would screw her even if they decided to get divorced and so she didn't understand why we had separate rooms. That just seemed crazy to me. Maybe I have Benjamin Button syndrome, am going through midlife crisis, or am simply seeing things as they are. I asked her to tell me why we live in an upside-down world.

But I didn't stop there.

I told her that I remembered when Lili was born, and I constantly wanted to hold her, touch her, and wouldn't put her in her own room to sleep. I brought her into Amir's and my bed, where she cuddled in my arms or simply slept on her father's chest. It was the sweetest sight. The same thing happened with Yasmin. I explained to Laura and Anna that everyone kept telling me what a great mistake it was because a child was supposed to sleep in his or her own bed I was spoiling my girls way too much, they said. Blah, blah, blah. *So*, I told them I said to myself, *okay, babies are supposed to sleep alone. After leaving their mothers' warm bodies with their mothers' heartbeats in their ears and their mothers' voices surrounding them for nine months, they now are forced into clothes and are supposed to sleep far away in a bed? Baby monitors substitute for mothers' ears?* Now don't get me wrong, I reminded them, I didn't constantly walk around with my babies and was Mrs. Mom incarnate.

I told Laura that it's so ironic because when those babies become teenagers and want to be left alone, we, the parents, become stalkers. We constantly ask them what was going on at school, check their bags, and look under their beds. We're supposed to spend time with them, but we don't get it: They don't want to spend time with us. Hello! We're the parents. Meaning we have no idea about anything.

I think they were following me then, and then I took it one step further.

I told Laura how I never understood why when people grow up and end up in a relationship, they sleep in one bed. I looked straight at Laura and asked her, "How many times have you wished you were alone? You might want to go to the bathroom in the middle of the night or get a glass of water, and it wakes up your partner. Or you like the room warm; he wants it cool. Or you might need to get up very early so you go to bed early, but he is a night person, climbing into bed way after you have fallen asleep. At this point every move in your own bed becomes a torture. You constantly have to worry about waking your partner. So, why do grown-ups, who, yes, might like all that touchy-feely stuff as well but mostly need a good sleep to be able to function the following day?"

I paused and waited for her response. She didn't give me one.

"Now don't say that that's just the way it is or for sex. That would disappoint me. If you have smaller kids in the house, you're too tired for sexual activity or too worried that someone might wake up and ruin the mood anyway. If you have grown-up kids who are either very independent or don't live in your house anymore, by that time people have usually forgotten how be close because they have been preoccupied with other things in their life."

"So what's your solution?" Laura asked, adding, "I have to have some testosterone around myself when I am in bed. Regardless of a good or bad sleep, and besides, gives me something to play with."

"Oh come on, Laura!" I said. "I personally think we should turn everything on its head. We hold a baby in our arms while he or she sleeps and as grown-ups live like the aristocratic families of the last century where you were married but basically lived in two different bedrooms in the same house. I think that's why the divorce rates were much lower then. It isn't because people couldn't get divorced but probably because they had their own life anyway. So, instead of putting a baby alone in a cold room, a grown-up should move in alone. That way you'll have your spouse and a good night's sleep. And besides, who said that you can only play with him at night? After a good sleep, you might be in the mood to practice playing during the day time! Ha ha!"

After I explained all of that to Ms. Laura Know-It-All, she just shut up.

March 10, 2006

Did you ever wonder what happens when kids become teenagers? I know I was one, but my parents are still alive, so it couldn't have been that bad. Sometimes I truly wonder if I'll survive my children's teenage years. Don't get me wrong I love both of them dearly even though they're so different personality-wise. But they have one thing in common: teenage life and hormonal rollercoasters.

Today I told Yasmin to clean up her things. Just the look on her face was worth millions. Okay at least she didn't practice screaming at me, and I didn't have to cover my ears.

Then I told Lili to pull down her shirt. Who invented those midriff-showing tops? I mean didn't the designer consider that the next generation of girls will have kidney problems because they showed their kidney/stomach area almost one hundred percent of the time? And what's with the low-cut necklines? All of their assets are hanging out. I still can't believe that my girls have boobs, which is a concern of mine. Of course, Lili didn't give me the silent treatment; she started yelling as if she was practicing an aria for the next opera.

"Why are you examining my body?" she snipped. "You have the dirtiest mind. Why are you looking at my belly anyway? Are you trying to tell me that I'm fat?"

I didn't even respond because I didn't get a chance as the accusations flew at me without pause. I wonder if these girls learn to use punctuation only when writing and not when speaking.

While I am in front of them, I have to act as the tough but loving mother. But when they behave like this, it truly breaks my heart. I feel so fragile. As I am looking at the screaming creature before me, I have flashbacks to their baby years. Sure, they screamed at that time, but only because they didn't have any other method of communication. But then they would calm down when I held them and rubbed their back. You can't hold and rub the back of a screaming teenager. It's not recommendable unless you are tired of your own life.

Sometimes I think it might be that they are bicultural and stand out. I'm trying to teach them the value of their heritage, but maybe they get completely mixed up? I mean when I was growing up, I had no idea to which group I belonged. Maybe they are going through the same dilemma. I mean as a teen you are stuck between childhood and adulthood and when you add in that you are French–Persian, you have four quarters to configure into your whole. My parents used the "good Persian girl" slogan on me, but I can't use it on them because the image has no reference. Through the Internet, they know about the rest of the world and, in a way, it makes all the differences between teenagers smaller. I guess it's good.

Didn't we want to eliminate cultural differences? Good, but what I should use as a motto now?

March 17, 2006

Okay, here is the deal: I don't speak the same language as men do. Don't laugh, I'm deadly serious! It took me close to thirty years to discover this. Yeah, I know, that's pretty late, but hey, better late than never.

Here's how I gained my wisdom:

Three weeks ago I found a long-lost friend online, and we e-mailed back and forth about all the things that had happened since we last spoke. Things like yes, I was still in the United States, and yes, he was still with the same company. Yes, he remembered my love for art and ballet, blah, blah, blah. He also remembered my *love* for noisette (nougat) pralines.

Then yesterday it happened: After sending him a text message and asking whether he was still in France (because I wanted him to send me a box of my favorite chocolate)—well, you know what, I'll re-create the conversation because it's way better to see it for yourself.

Me: "So are you still in France?"

Him: "Indeed, but not for much longer."

Me: "So do you have any nougat?"

Him: "I don't know that it can be called nougat? Do you want me to eat it?"

Me: "Are you serious? That's my favorite! What's your favorite?" (I know this is a cheesy question!)

Him: "Now I don't understand what you are saying at all! Are you really talking about chocolate?"

Me: "Why? What did you think I meant?"

Well, after I hit the send button, a light bulb went off, and I understood what he thought I was saying. I didn't know whether to laugh and roll on the floor about his naïve, yet dirty fantasy or to get offended. I decided to replay over and over the whole e-mail exchange in my head.

These kinds of conversations had happened to me before, but it was the first time that I noticed a certain pattern. Why was it that men always liked to come on to me? Was I acting, talking, or doing something provocative? Yes, I used to be a master in flirting, but that was a long time ago. Even my own mother has noticed that I have become so serious and mature, so that can't be it. Then I realized that usually these types of conversations happen after they see me—in person or a picture of me. Is it my looks?

I can assure that I dress very modestly. Even for as liberal as I am, I have some very old-fashioned ideas and I conduct myself as very knowledgeable and smart. In society, people actually consider me intelligent and good-looking.

When I compare myself to other women I know, I have concluded that when a woman is nice looking and has some brains, it's too much for a man to handle. A guy has two categories for women: beautiful and brainy. One equals sex goddess; the other equals nerd. Men imagine that a woman who cares about her looks does so only to attract men; he wants sex. And that's kind of our fault. We encouraged that mode of thinking. I guess no guy ever thought that women might dress up just because they want to. To get back to this incident, I guess my friend thought the same about me after seeing my picture again. He thought that someone like me was looking for a man.

I used to think that I wouldn't understand Persian men because they have bad tempers and are somewhat macho. But now, I truly believe that when it comes to all men, regardless of age, nationality etc., there should be a seventh sort of intelligence: gender intelligence. Men and women do speak different languages! Hey, now I might be one step ahead of everyone: I learned my first word in male-speak: Nougat means sex!

March 21, 2006

It's Persian New Year (*Nowruz*)! Stemming from the times of the Zoroastrians, *Nowruz* is translated to mean "a New Day." It's such a beautiful concept. The whole celebration starts with the arrival of the equinox. What I love the most is that everyone was so excited. There was a real feeling of a new beginning, all being lead by nature. Birds would sing, flowers would blossom, and even animals knew what was happening because the equinox marks the end of winter and the beginning of spring. It's a little different every year.

I remember as a little girl listening to my grandmother tell stories from when she was young. Although she claimed the gathering was on a smaller scale, the day was celebrated in a grand manner with all her children, meaning my aunts and uncles, cousins and their families, coming to her house. It showed their respect to celebrate the new beginning of the year with her. Everyone would gather at the eldest family member's house, wearing their new clothes and having the newest hairstyles- all for the beginning of the New Year. The older family members would give the children *'Eidi'*, basically money instead of presents. These were new gold coins or money bills, still warm from the printer. The children would get excited and start counting how much each got, comparing and begging the older one's for more in order to compete among each other.

I explained the famous seven 'S's table to Lili and Yasmin and even have the table in our home as a way to keep the tradition alive. But it's really difficult because we don't have relatives here. (It makes it difficult to be the "different" ones.) I try to explain to them that in the same way my parents continued with the Persian traditions for me,

I want to keep it and pass it on to them, so that they can pass it down to their children. It might not work because I'm only Persian by blood, not necessarily in behavior.

Yasmin's friend came over and saw the table. Of course, Yasmin wanted to drag her away; she was embarrassed. The funny thing is that her friend wanted to know more about it, so I started explaining each item on the table had a specific meaning for the Persian New Year.

Sabzeh—green sprout to reflect rebirth

Serkeh—vinegar to reflect age and wisdom

Sīr—garlic to reflect health

Samanu—sweet and sour berries to reflect love

Sīb—an apple to reflect health

Sekkeh—coins to reflect wealth

Somaq—sumac berry powder to reflect spice in your life

Yasmin's friend thought it was very interesting and beautiful.

When the girls left to go downtown, I started thinking about the time I spent as a child in France. Had I been as embarrassed because I was different and for celebrating different holidays in addition to the French ones? Probably yes. Is it only with age that you realize that being different is not as bad as you thought? Eventually you see that you can stand out and actually take advantage of that fact, not in a negative way, of course, but putting your uniqueness to a good cause.

Just think about it. Aren't we all human in the end? Who told us that we have to speak this certain language and behave a certain way? Aren't those all manmade boundaries? Of course, all the while we're trying to teach our kids to think outside the box. Something about the entire picture bothers me. Instead of embracing the differences, we point them out and create confusion by saying be different but not different like that.

How was I raised? We always celebrated all events, so my brother, Sam, and I didn't feel like outsiders in the family or among our friends. Did it work? Not really. Don't laugh but I thought of myself as a tulip. Tulips were originally from the Middle East but were brought to the Netherlands, but now everyone thinks of tulips as Dutch. Now imagine you take a tulip and bring it to Spain. After the first year, you probably wouldn't see any difference in it, but as time passes, the tulip changes. Eventually someone looks at the so-called Spanish tulips and says, "Hey, the tulips in Spain are so different from the ones in the Netherlands." But they're still tulips, which is my point. I might be from a country, I've changed throughout the years, but my blood is the same. I'm one of those Spanish tulips.

I guess regardless of how you look at it, parents try to teach their children two or more cultures, but it will always be difficult—except if they have their kids associate with others who are in the same situation. I think the issue is that kids of a certain age don't want to be different from the outside world. They don't care about traditions or culture because for them culture is what goes on at school. It's up to us parents to give them some sort of insight into their ancestors, so that hopefully one day they might voluntarily explore it. They might come to see it as an asset to their unique identity instead of just a difference.

March 22, 2006

I spoke to Sam today; the funny thing is we always talk about our childhood memories around *Nowruz*. Today I told him about this one girl, whose name I had forgotten, who had always pinched me at every Nowruz event at our aunt's house. I had no idea why—until today because Sam actually had known this whole time. I can't believe that my brother knew some girly gossip. He said that the girl had been always jealous of me and the fact that I spoke French. Her mom had told her that she should see me as an example because I was smart and spoke two languages. I don't know if the mom was right or wrong in her assessment. I guess thank you for the compliment, but why on earth do you have to tweak your own kid and have her hate me? Huh? Do you know how many pinches I got because of your pep talk? I could probably sue her. Ha ha!

It's so interesting to see how much your childhood actually shapes your adult life. People always smile and make fun of psychiatrists about asking, "How was your childhood?" But when you think about it, it makes sense.

Childhood is somewhat the mud phase and no matter how the outside world treats you, your mud will be shaped by something. After you grow into adulthood and harden into dry mud, even though we never really completely dry up, it's much more difficult to change your shape. I guess you could use some water to moisten the mud again. But what would be the water in the adulthood? Maybe it's the people around you, or depending on the shape you're in, how life in general treats you. But the funny thing is the longer the mud stays in one shape, the more it will crumble and lose its original contour when you try to change its shape. I guess it's the same with people. The older we are, the more difficult it becomes for us to change. Isn't that the Lewis change model: unfreeze, change, refreeze? It's pretty much the same, except that I believe that the refreezing in my sample has more to do with remodeling than with crumbling.

Anyway, the whole time I was wondering why on earth that girl didn't like me, she saw me as a threat, probably as an unknown force that took her mom's attention and love away from her. I'll have to ask my mom if she still knows that family. I would like to know how that girl, now a woman, would react hearing my name. Maybe she'd pinch me again.

March 23, 2006

You know what one of the weirdest things is? That parenting is one of the most thankless, yet most wonderful things in this world. Does that make sense?

Yasmin and Lili drive me insane at times. What do I expect? They are two teenage girls, and yes, they are more similar to me than I would like to admit: rebellious, headstrong, stubborn, and challenging, yet sweet and unpredictable. We were getting ready to go to the New Year party, which Amir always disliked, but the girls *do* like. Go figure! They try to forget about their Persianness all year long and only think about it at one event. I guess this was what I meant when I said they liked being with people their own age who have the same bicultural dilemma.

Anyway, we were getting ready, and there was this big World War III in the bathroom about mascara and lipstick. Yes, these are the really important issues these days. I had to laugh, which didn't help make peace among the wounded parties. But I just visualized them as babies and how I would have reacted if someone had fast-forwarded to these scenes.

I believe that it's more challenging to have teenage daughters than sons. Sure, sons give you other joys and headaches; you worry about motorcycles and probably more about the fact that they aren't as open and extroverted as girls are, making it much more difficult to find out what goes on in their minds.

Seeing the girls growing older and having these kinds of fights makes me realize that not only am I aging, but also this is all part of life. The ups and downs will shape them. I guess that's the molding part.

While I was looking at them in high heels and mascara, I had flashbacks to their kindergarten years. Don't ask me why, but suddenly I thought of the first time each of them didn't want to hold my hand in public and pulled her tiny hand out of mine. I was so sad, so heartbroken, as I thought that I was loosing my babies—not my girls, but the babyness of them. They didn't need me to protect them so openly now. Looking at them made me realize that they're still very much babies on the inside and they still need to know that I'm there when they need me *and* when they don't want me to be. I guess then, I'll have to disappear.

As I mentioned earlier, letting go of my hand marked the second cutting of their umbilical cord, and that cord always grows back in different shapes, is recut, and is reformed. Now they want to know that I've started to look at them as independent equals.

Once I read somewhere that we have to give our kids wings to fly and roots to know from where they come. In a couple of years, they'll be out of school and go off to college. They'll be physically gone, but what about mentally? I think by that time they will have been shaped enough to know that they do have roots and that no matter what happens, there is someone who loves them unconditionally. Their umbilical cord will be in shape of phone calls, occasional e-mails occasionally, or a home visit with a warm meal and freshly done laundry.

April 1, 2006

There's still nothing on the job front. I'm just tired of everything—all these years of studying, emancipating, and dreaming big. What now?

No one in school prepares you for the bad times. They constantly teach you the breaking points of this, breaking points of that; market this, market that; and draw this, draw that. But do they actually teach you: "Hey, you guys, you might be going through all the classes and end up having a 4.0 GPA, but guess what—when economy sucks, it simply sucks and you won't be getting a job."

Maybe I should go back to school; it seems like that was the only place I was able to succeed anyway. And you know why? Because it reflected and visualized an ideal world. It was a fantasy world where all the drawings were perfect even though we knew that no artist is ever satisfied with their painting, all the cases were solved to everyone's satisfaction, and everything was well balanced. Did anyone actually teach you how to apply this knowledge?

Lately everyone has been telling me, "You should open your own business!" If I hear that "perfect recommendation" one more time, I won't be able to control my reaction. I mean seriously! What if I work in a genre where there is so much competition—and I'm talking at the genius level—that becoming your own boss would be more a nightmare than a sweet dream? What if I have to support my family and simply can't afford risking it all? The media always tells us about the Larry Ellisons and Bill Gateses. Yes, they made it. But if you read their stories, you'll quickly realize that both of them where single men when they slept in a corner and had the pizza boxes pile up like the leaning tower of Pisa.

I do find jobs, and I have interviews. Here people aren't allowed to ask me whether I have children, but there must be something in my look that gives it away when they ask, "Is it an issue if you have to work eighty hours a week?" or even better, "This job requires six days a week of traveling."

I know some women do this. There's one woman from Lili's ballet studio who left her four kids with her ex and went back into the work force. Is that selfish? I don't know.

The fact is that I'm just tired—tired of looking for the right fit, of being rejected, of waiting, and, yes, of being tired. Plus, this whole job hunt is creating more stress with Amir. His constant nagging about why I have to work and what's wrong with staying at home and taking care of the kids makes me want to strangle him. The kids don't need my constant attention like they did when they were babies; I don't have to follow them around and sit at home. But they still need me enough to where I can't travel six days a week. I guess I'm not making sense to him.

I don't even know what I want. I wonder if the other moms who don't have to work but want to feel the same. I wonder if they look at their kids, who are slowly but surely cutting their umbilical cords and having their insider talks, and then look at themselves in the mirror every morning and every evening and think, *What about me? Where are my dreams? Where did I stop existing?*

I love my kids more than anything in this world, but Amir simply doesn't get that when the kids are gone, it's going to be me in an empty house without anything onto which to hold. I'll probably sit in front of the calendar and mark the days when they come back from college so I can buy enough detergent for their laundry and precook food for them. Is that the outcome of all those long nights of studying, running from class to class, and challenging the professors?

What happened to *me*? What happened to *me*?

April 2, 2006

Okay, so now I have no idea what to do. Yeah, I know, imagine *me* being speechless and without a wise-crack answer.

Lili came home and asked me if she could have a boyfriend. I asked her if someone had asked her out. She said, "Well, there's this boy, who told my friend that he really liked me and that she shouldn't tell me." I guess in boy-talk that means, "Please let her know that I'm so, so interested in her and would like to go out with her." So the friend came and told Lili.

And here she was, asking me.

Uhhhh!

I asked her if she liked him, too. She said, "Yeah, he's kind of hot." But she gave a warning look that I shouldn't ask any more questions, which confused me. She came to me, for which I'm very thankful, because most girls wouldn't even ask. Then she gave me a situation and expected an answer based on the motto, "Give me an answer, a solution! I want it, and I want it now."

No questions allowed, and I wonder why. Probably because she wants to keep it as objective as possible. When I ask questions, she has to—heaven forbid—admit in front of her mother that she has feelings for someone. This would make the entire situation oh-so disgusting!

I said, "It's only normal to find the opposite sex—"

At that point she said, "Mom, don't make it disgusting!"

Okay, I thought, *Well, that door got closed pretty fast; let me try something else.* So I said, "If you like him, have a head on your shoulders, and know when to say, 'No,' why not?"

She looked at me and replied as she left the room with a huge smile, "Okay, and why didn't you say so half an hour ago?"

After she had left, I felt that she only wanted to test me to see what I would say. I guess it was not a question whether she could have sex or not. Funny how as a mother I always think about the extreme, instead of the question as it is. I guess many of these kids only talk more about sex? If so, then why do so many of these girl-kids—that's what they are after all—already have sexual experiences, especially when they have no idea what sex is? Sure, they know about the physical act but do they even think as far as the emotional aspect of it? I guess some parents are so closed up and put their kids in such a tight box, that they don't consider that hormones will eventually kick in and questions will arise. That's what I don't get. Why not talk to kids instead of trying to hide the entire topic from them? I'd rather have my girls ask me questions about penises than checking one out. Not that I could show them one, but I want them to find out about it from me rather than getting the wrong information on the Internet or asking someone who probably knows less than they do.

And please don't give me the excuse that some parents don't feel comfortable talking about such subjects. If you consider yourself mature enough to have sex, just suck it up and be mature enough to raise your child. Don't suddenly become a saint and pretend you had your kids while maintaining your innocence.

The fact is that our kids do grow up, and yes as parents we do make tons of mistakes, for which they will blame us later on. (The same way we blame our parents in our shrink's office.) But hey, embrace every change and accept the fact that you might screw up. It's better to make a mistake while trying to do the right thing than to remain silent and have your child do the wrong thing. It makes fewer wrinkles, too, you know. ☺

Okay, now I better get some sleep; it's going to be a long day tomorrow. Good night.

April 25, 2006

Lately there's been all this talk about sexuality and sensuality with Amir. I don't even know what he knows and what he wants. He looks at the human body like a piece of something—not even meat. I miss being seen and being made love to during sex. And when I tell him this, he snaps that I have lesbian dreams.

I admit that I've had them. Because I believe that only a woman can understand a woman's body and know her by heart. And also, a woman would take the time to discover and patiently make sure her partner enjoys the physical contact as well. I had fantasies; now I only have dreams. But trying to explain this to this man would be beyond my abilities and strength. It's like talking to a little child and trying to explain Einstein's theories.

I wanted to shake him and tell him to take off my clothes and discover me. "Don't just rip the lingerie off but look at me. Look at the lace and the ribbons as part of the whole and slowly work your way to the reward." I wanted to tell him that I hated his lovemaking because it wasn't lovemaking. I felt more like a cheap whore when he was with me. I want him to understand me, look at me, and wait until I also climax.

He pretends he feels so bad for me and says that it's my own fault because I hate to lose control and that's why I can't have an orgasm. I wanted to scream!

For me the female orgasm is truly a mystery. I heard it could be great, but there must be a reason why it mostly happens through stimulation of the clitoris and not through vaginal stimulation. I read about it in a magazine. And yes, I even looked it up online. But what all these smart people don't understand, which is absolutely clear to *me*, is there must be a certain trust with the partner to let go of control. There must be a certain connection, mentally or physically to totally release yourself. I need to be comfortable in his presence to let go and let him see me climax.

And that's exactly the missing piece: I don't. He has said so many things and treated me so badly at times that I can't. Maybe, yes, it's my own issue. It's like I get this mental block that won't let me get to that point because I don't want to give him the satisfaction of being able to say, "Hey, I made her scream of pleasure!" And he would, too.

What I did try to tell him is that there was a huge difference between lovemaking and sex. Sex for me is only the physical act. You can pay someone for sex. But lovemaking is the mental aspect behind it, which is more than the hormonal urge. You can never pay someone to make love to you.

He just doesn't get it.

I tried to tell him that after being with him, I would wait for him to fall asleep, go sit on the bathroom floor, and cry for a while because I felt so empty and lonely. While he would have a facial expression of 'Mission Accomplished', put on his clothes and sit behind the TV and start his channel surfing. He did not notice or did not care to see what I would do after he left me alone in bed. So many times I had heard about how women actually enjoyed the spooning afterwards. Never got to experience it myself.

April 26, 2006

This whole sexuality thing is still on my mind. Right now I'm not having sex, so it's better to just think about it. That's pretty logical to me.

I've grown up with the motto: "A good Iranian girl doesn't have premarital sex." This wasn't a question, or a statement; it was as sure as the *sura* in the Koran. One hundred years ago, a woman had to be this, and it just wouldn't change. My family has a very modern stance on women when it comes to education, etc., but when it came to sex, like in many Iranian families, it just discussed behind closed doors if at all.

And this would have been fine if the men had been treated the same way. I always asked my mother—because you talk to her about these things because although she might not always admit it, she didn't believe in the nonsense of the good Iranian girl either—why are couples supposed to have a relationship at the "kitchen table," as I love to call it, and not in bed when a lot is at stake? Don't they say that a man will promise you the world and actually keep his word within the five minutes right after his orgasm? So shouldn't that be the place where all the negotiations in a relationship should be done? Then why shouldn't I talk to the man in that place before signing a lifelong matrimonial contract? Well, like many of my questions regarding the Iranian tradition and religion, these stay unanswered as well.

Recently my mom told me that the trend in Iran has changed now. Thank you! After so many generations of women lost in this tradition, now men like it when their future wives have sexual experience. Good! If a man has been with several women and they have given him a sampling of their gifts, does that make him a pimp? No. And that's exactly why an adult woman shouldn't be seen as a whore if she has had several relationships.

My current problems are all the result of this old way of thinking. For so many years I was told to guard my virginity and that, my husband, the first man in my life, would appreciate that. Of course, I was scared at the time. I'd had biology, which gave me some idea of what to expect, but I'd never seen a real naked man in my life. I had no idea how a man's penis looks erected—except I watched a couple of soft porn movies once, but it didn't show the whole thing.

Do you know what happened when Amir found out that I was a virgin? His first reaction was worse than anything I could describe. Telling me that no woman should be a virgin after the age of 18, since that was an indication that no man ever wanted her. Saying that it was a complete turn-off to find out that I had no practical experience and that my sexual phantasies were only in theory. Can you believe it? All my life I was told one thing, and then he, a man I truly loved at that time, tells me that due to this fact, it doesn't work.

Sometimes I try to get over the past, forget about everything, thinking that the past is history and that it only creates a base for the present and enjoy the moment to create a good foundation for the future. But how do you forget these things? How can you forget that you kept yourself one way for this one man and that he rejected you so many times? That's probably why I don't like to be with him and I've never enjoyed my sex life. They usually say that having sex with your partner is supposed to be a stress reliever. But in my case it always brings back the bad memories of those early bedroom experiences.

I honestly think that the reason people say that women should stay virgins is because they are worried about the women's strength. Really, women are empowered through their sexuality and gain a certain power over men.

That's what Amir doesn't like. He believes the whole women's movement was ridiculous and that woman should know where their place is and stay there. That would include sex, too. He says the whole lovey-dovey stuff doesn't work for him. He calls it "emotional garbage." In his world a woman should be ready for sex when the man wants it and then miraculously disappear. It's basically the moon syndrome. (Didn't Charlie Sheen say that men don't pay women for sex but to go away after sex?) Amir says that love and sexuality are two different things—no kidding!—*but* when he loves a woman, he isn't able to have sex with her.

I just don't get it. I try telling him that sex is the physical way of expressing your feelings for a person. I guess he isn't used to a woman asking about sex and talking about it—another example of an Iranian man, who takes things for granted.

April 27, 2006

I was talking to Judy who just lost her job. It's terrible! The poor thing was at work one day, and her boss came in and said that the company was in a bad financial position. He told her that they needed to close the doors. They got their last paycheck two days later, and after that it was good luck.

I guess no one should be surprised, with the economy being as it is. But when you read about it in the papers, it doesn't have a personal touch. Judy is a very talented woman; she has so many assets and could add tremendously to any company. Listening to her makes my situation so real again.

Amir doesn't get it. I told him about Judy, and he just says that women shouldn't be working outside the home and if they do, it should be a smaller job.

"What do you mean by that?" I asked.

"You know, just a small job to keep her busy and out of trouble," he explained. I couldn't believe it.

I think it's because he wants to make sure that the woman is always financially dependent. But what I don't understand is that these men who want their wives to be the financial dependent complain about their wives spending too much.

"So what would you do if I asked you to pay for all my expenses?" I shot back.

He gave me a weird look and answered, "You shouldn't have expenses."

"Why?"

"Because you should be busy taking care of the house and kitchen."

Can you believe it? When I say that this man doesn't belong in this century, people laugh at me and think I'm only joking.

Okay, so back to Judy. I'm not sure what her plans are now. She is clueless, too. Jim left her a couple of years ago, and since then she has always been an independent woman. She has her house and the kids. But financially, regardless of her ex-husband's alimony check, she really needs a job and a paycheck. I told her to take a short break and then start looking. But I doubt that she'll be able to sit still for a day.

April 29, 2006

Today I decided to stop by Judy's for support. It was amazing what she told me! I had no idea that Judy and her family had financial issues. It turns out that she was making decent money but had invested all of it in her house—you know, remodeling, renovating, and stuff. Now she told me that she would only able to afford two more mortgages payments without her income.

"What?" I said shocked. "What are your plans after that?"

"I've started to look around, and I'll just have to take anything to bolster my income. Worst case, I'll have to sell the house in a short sale, in order to avoid a foreclosure."

"But how are you planning to convince the bank to wait?" I inquired.

"I still have some savings and already told the bank about my situation," she explained. "The housing market's fine, so I should be able to find some buyers very soon. Jim feels bad, but you know how he is. He just doesn't want to get involved. He made it very clear that it isn't his problem anymore."

"I guess we're just going to have move to Florida. His parents are there, and they've offered to help. We'll see what happens next."

I told her to let me know if she needed anything. These stories just break my heart. It must be devastating. At least his parents are nice to her even though he left her.

Oh and today Judy told me the story behind his takeoff. I'm so happy that I can at least write it down because I gave her my word that I wouldn't tell anyone. Jim, whom I only met once, was bisexual and left her for another man.

What's shocking to me is not his sexual orientation—I don't care into whom a man sticks his penis. The fact is he never told her about it, was married for such a long time, had three kids with her, and wham! "Oh sorry, honey," he said. "I'm screwing around on you—with another guy." Are you fucking kidding me? You couldn't have possibly said from the beginning that you liked screwing both sexes? Maybe Judy would have walked away, knowing that women weren't her only competition and she had to compete with men as well.

As I was leaving I thought, *Why do the worst things always happen to the nicest people? Don't we always preach that good things happen to good people? But I guess they're so patient and even smile during the worst misery, so we smile as well and think that everything be fine.*

It will be fine, right?

May 9, 2006

Today is Mommy's Day!

I was at the mall today to pick up a couple of things for my girls, and I noticed, because I had never noticed before, all the advertising for Mother's Day. This year all the store windows advertised that on that specific day you had to give your mother something. It disgusted me. You had to buy her flowers, a new Pottery Barn picture frame, or this or that.

Why? Well, it's all a marketing trick. If you don't follow the crowd, you'll feel terrible as though you don't love your mother, right? The Web sites talk about all the best and the worst gifts you can get your mother. And, of course, everyone reads them and follows. In the back of your mind is the list of all the items you purchased in previous years, and heaven forbid you get her something twice in a row.

While all these thoughts were crossing my mind, I thought about what the inventor of Mother's Day, Anna Marie Jarvis, had said after she noticed what had happened to her idea to appreciate mothers. She hated the fact that the whole industry took advantage of people by manipulating them to feel good when they bought some flowers or any other item for their moms. Sure, I'm a woman, and I love getting flowers, the more the better. I love Pottery Barn picture frames; I love clothes, etc.

Look at what I did this year. Every year I always send my mother flowers or plants—from the United States to Europe. I call up her florist and order them. The florist lady still gets excited when she hears my voice, calling her from the US. My mom loves the flowers, roses and orchids are her favorites, and when I would go over to visit, she would show me her garden and which plants had arrived this year. But this year my mom is on a business trip right now and she'll return in a couple of days, so I decided not to send the flowers. Instead, I figured I would wait until I saw her and then buy them for her. Then I realized something, *As much as she loves the orchids, maybe she is waiting for something else.* Today she called me from the road and I told her how much I missed her, and regardless of the distance, no matter whether she was at her home or on a trip, I felt so lonely without her being at home. I told her how much I missed calling her first thing in the morning and that her geographical distance upset me, and I really noticed it now. I told her that I couldn't wait for her to get home and that I had no idea how I would survive if I didn't hear her voice or feel her presence. My mother laughed, and I could feel the love in her laughter. She was so grateful to hear that from me; I believe not even one hundred orchids could have expressed that kind of love, respect, and gratitude for her.

I think after being my mother's daughter for thirty-four years and being a mom for fourteen years, I understand what Mother's Day is all about. It's not about another vase on the kitchen table, another shirt in her closet, or another book on her nightstand—those things a mother can buy herself. Mother's Day isn't about relieving your conscience; it's about expressing to your mother how you feel about her.

I'm grateful to my mother for carrying me for nine months, giving birth to me, watching over my bed when I was little, caring about me when I was sick, waiting for me to return home from school, being excited and sad with me, crying with me and pushing me not to give up, and for laughing with me. I'm thankful for her just being there for me every time I call her. I love her more than words could possibly express!

To all the mothers in the world, no matter how young or old and no matter from which great nation of this world, Happy Mother's Day!

May 16, 2006

I read an awful story today in a magazine about female genital cutting, or female genital mutilation. It's the real life story of a young girl from Togo. She fled her country to escape this tribal custom for young girls, who usually have no idea what is happening to them. These girls are usually held by their mothers, older sisters, aunts, or other close female relatives, while the cutting party is between their legs to cut of most or parts of their outer genitals. Now to clarify this issue from the beginning, this isn't an Islamic rule. It's based on tribal law, which is usually applied in African countries for numerous other reasons. (They want to protect women, to make the woman look clean, or to make intercourse painful for women so they won't cheat on their husbands.)

I hadn't heard about this practice until a couple of years ago when I heard about the "Desert Flower," another real life story of a young girl escaping her African country. Personally I'm completely against this practice, not because what they do, but because of how they do it. I respect other countries' laws and customs, *but*, and here's where the big but comes, it can't put health in danger and must respect humanity. This custom usually is done with dirty and rusty razor blades or broken glass pieces. Women and girls sometimes die due to heavy bleeding after the ritual or later during childbirth. That doesn't even take into account the pain they'll have during sex or menstruation.

Now on the other end of the spectrum, a couple of days ago, I read in a medical magazine about female genital plastic surgery. I'm not sure, but I think I'm living on Mars. I have heard of people increasing or decreasing their bust sizes or their butt sizes; tucking their tummies; increasing or decreasing their lips or noses; or lifting their eyes, etc., but plastic surgery on your private parts?

The article immediately got my attention. I was curious that someone would actually have an opinion about how my private parts look. Well, to enlighten you if you were as virgin like as me on this topic: Women increase the size of the outer labia, decrease the size of their inner ones, change the size of their clitorises, and/or alter the shape of the entire part. *Okay,* I thought as I made sure the magazine didn't fall out of my hands, *There are plastic surgeons who specialize in this area.* And then I read the "Why Do This Surgery" part. The reason stated was because it looks nicer and cleaner and is supposed to enhance sexual desire. "Oh-kay," I said, "Now you tell me: What's the difference between these two cases?"

One is done in African countries, the other in the West. If you answered that, ding, ding, ding, you win the first prize. But I hate to tell you that that isn't all. The second similarity is that they are both done for aesthetic reasons. So why do we fight against genetic cutting and for women's rights in Africa but advertise for a woman's right to plastic surgery to alter female genitalia in the Western world? From what I understand it's done in both places for the beauty of women and sexual reasons and done to the same general area of the body. Here it is for pleasure; there it is for pain. Here women decide on their own to undergo this surgery and accept the pain they might have later; there the girls are mostly forced in having a "surgery." That's the key difference!

Why did I put the last word in quotations? Here, the procedure is done in a sterile environment in a hospital, antibiotics are taken, and the woman is told to rest, not to have sex for up to four weeks afterward, and not to lift anything heavy. There, a woman has the cuts done in public places, is held down by a woman she trusts, and doesn't have any sedation. She actually feels every second of the pain, has no antibiotics, and is under no restrictions after the procedure. But all that aside, the most important reason is freedom of choice. A woman has the freedom to decide what is done to her body. Here, a woman volunteers, and there, she is forced.

I believe the countries that believe in female genital cutting should enforce their tribal laws and pass it as a statutory law to mandate the safety and preserve her rights. If the procedure is legal, it can be required to be done at a hospital. Additionally, creating a consenting age requirement would allow these girls to decide whether they want to give their genitals that particular beauty boost. It should all be about the safety and freedom of women. How about putting that on the top of the priority list?

May 25, 2006

Guess what? Guess what? The last place where I had an interview—the good one!—called me today and—*I'm hired!* They told me about the salary, which as a matter of Persian pride I had to negotiate, pretending that their company couldn't possibly survive without me. I said they would need to increase the salary just a tiny bit—and they did.

I'm so, so excited!!! I can't wait to go back to work on June 1!

June 1, 2006

I had my first day at the new job! It's so exciting. The people there were very nice and welcoming—so different from the last place. I guess the four months of waiting was really worth it. I told you that everything turns out for the best in the end. Well, I really didn't say that, but who cares? The fact is that I'm very, very happy right now.

Oh, I completely forgot that I'm having twenty guests over in two days, and I have to start my preparations. Wish me good luck! I don't even know what to cook and don't really want to have a caterer. Four months without work really sucked the life out of my purse.

But hey, I'm on the way up again, so no looking back!

So what should I cook for my guests? It has to be something that I can prepare a day or so in advance.

Amir is probably—no, most likely—not going to be there for it. He has never showed up with me for events and hates it when we have guests, so why should he stay now?

In a way, it still breaks my heart to look at him. What happens to people? I read that statistically fifty percent, if not more, of marriages end up in a divorce. *Hm,* I thought, *why not post this in a wedding planner's office?* I wonder how hard it would hit their business.

I always wondered why people, not only the bride but many men as well, make such a fuss about of their wedding day. Add the divorce statistic to that, and the other fifty percent should start saving for the eventual separation on the wedding day. It's kind of like saying to their guests, "Eat everything on your plate! I paid for it! And I will get a divorce while I'm still paying for this fucking event!"

And please don't give me that "It's only one day in your life!" nonsense. Most men and women get remarried, so with wedding costs as high as $60,000 per wedding, it will bring the total to $120,000 per person. Oh, wait—then actually, the higher divorce rates help the wedding planers! Hah, I love my smart-ass math skills. I wonder if wedding planners plan a cheap wedding to make sure the people end up at their place again.

Well, anyway, enough of this. I still need to figure what I'll be cooking.

June 14, 2006

Today was one of the weirdest days. I went to work, which I truly love! I still can't believe that I was able to find this perfect job, with a nice boss, great hours, and everything. Well, anyway, the funniest thing happened on one of the networking sites to which I had subscribed. A guy sent me an e-mail, asking me if I knew a certain person. One e-mail led to another, and we went back and forth until by the end of the day, it had become a long chain. It was so random.

I don't know I have this feeling about him. He seems very nice, but you never know over e-mail. His name is Steven; he is an investment banker and into sports. I'll find out more and let you know.

That reminds me—I wonder what happened to Ben. He disappeared off planet Earth. Well, I didn't ever e-mail him back.

I discovered something else today. You know how everyone always says that chocolate is the answer? I'm so excited to admit that I discovered a dessert with fewer calories. It tastes so extremely good, and the kids love it, too. I took ramekins and placed an apple ring inside each one, topped it off with frozen berries, and then put dough made of butter, egg, milk, sugar, and flour on top of that. I guess it's some sort of cobbler? But this was much, much better. I'm so proud of myself! He he he!

June 15, 2006

I had at least ten e-mails from this Steven guy. It was nothing specific, just the usual let's-talk-and-meet line. But hello, I'm at work and can't sit by my BlackBerry the entire time. I told him that we could have lunch tomorrow.

June 16, 2006

Okay- so I had lunch with Mr. Steven. He is very tall and attractive, wore office casual clothes and had the brightest smile one could imagine.

'Hmm', I thought, *'Nice eye candy!'*

We only had an hour lunch time, so after the usual introduction, we started talking about the networking sites and work in general. He does commercial real estate, he said. "Interesting!", I responded. I thought that this explained the bright smile. Typical sales man. Haha!

"Sometimes I have clients, who like to work with me for their personal real estate as well. That's the best reward, since it shows how much they trust me." he said.

I had a salad with some shrimps, and was delighted that he didn't try to talk me into ordering for me or asking me why I didn't eat a steak. While I was pleased, I am not sure. Something is bothering me. Can't put a finger on it though. But I hope to see him again.

June 17, 2006

Steven is so sweet. He still sends me at least ten e-mails a day and calls me twice a day. I guess I like the attention. Yeah, I *do* like the attention.

Today he said —after e-mailing me for two days only!—"I've been waiting all my life for a woman like you." Isn't that the nicest thing?

After work, I had to stop at the grocery store, get some other things at another store, and pick up some plants to do some weekend gardening. I had called the kids and told them that I might be an hour late. At first I thought, *They might be upset about not having any dinner.* But what surprise! When I got home, they had already done their homework, cleaned up after themselves, and brought the garbage out; Lili was making dinner while Yasmin was doing dishes. It was so wonderful! Such a sight filled my heart with joy, as I watched my kids get along so beautifully—maybe only for an hour but hey, that's at least something!

It was the cutest thing ever as I saw Lili try to teach Yasmin how to do the dishes right.

Lili said, "You are simply a clueless child, Yasmin. You should learn from me, you older sister."

I chuckled and said, "Ah, sibling order never changes."

I thought, *It's just like Sam and me; he still sees at me as his little sister.*

You know, birth order makes a huge difference in our attitudes toward life, and it's mostly shaped by parenting. The older ones have the burden of "breaking the way" responsibility. They're responsible for the parents' rule-setting, and their role is to define the rules because parents aren't born parents. I know I learn as I go, and many times, I have no idea whether the rules and boundaries I set are too strict or loose.

Sometimes I use my own parents as role models for parenting, and other times, I want to do exactly the opposite of what they did with me. It's so difficult to keep your love for your kids in balance with the rules they need to follow, to counter your pride in them with the expectations of what they need to achieve, and also to know how much to release yet still stay present in your kids' lives.

Like I mentioned earlier, I think there should be a class about parenting. I know there are some classes and books that tell you what you are supposed to do. But these are only some broad, confusing guidelines that can't be used in every specific situation because every child and every parent is different.

I just have to make mistakes and learn as I go. But instead of seeing the mistakes I made, I should be honest about them and see them as assets.

Back to Steven, it's so refreshing to hear all these words. I guess regardless of all the false steps, I'm still a woman after all.

June 18, 2006

That's it! I'll kill this man! Today he blamed me for his bad day. Hello! We didn't even see each other.

It started this morning when he couldn't find his workout clothes. I don't care where you put your stinking stuff. Go and die. Why do you blame me for everything?

I just can't stand his voice. Yeah, It's the voice that used to whisper all of those sweet things into my ear. But now all I hear is screaming.

I just want to kick him. His whole existence drives me insane. It turned out that he had put his stuff into the laundry room to dry. Ha ha ha! Go screw yourself.

Well, that was a good start to the day. Then around lunch he send me an email, telling me what an unorganized woman I was. *'Oh just shut up!'* I thought. Continuing with the fact that Yasmin had some issue in Math and I probably didn't even know that! I just replied to his email "Check your credit card statement, you actually paid for the tutor and we even spoke about her issues and YOU don't remember!' He replied, but I didn't open up his email. What's the use? Reading more about what a monstrous person I was?

That night, the girls had so much homework. Considering that the school year ends in a week, apparently the schools try to push all that knowledge into the student's brains. Why do I feel like I never left school? I don't remember if my mother had to sit next to me while I worked as well, cracking the whip.

Hey, that inspired a thought. Maybe Amir's into the whipping game? Grrr, that's so not my style. I wonder how people do it. I guess it's true sex, no emotional or romantic shit. It's just pure sex to satisfy yourself.

You know, there was this guy at the airport once who told me straightforward that he wanted me to be his mistress. Maybe I should give him a call? I was way too chicken then. I guess inside I'm still like my grandmother, trying to please society.

June 20, 2006

I can't believe the day I had. Any working mom would probably sympathize with me: I had to take the girls to school because they both had to be there earlier for a science project. Then I had to take two hours off of work to take Yasmin to her dance class, come home to help Lili with her homework, then go and pick Yasmin up because she had a two-hour break, then drive her back to the studio again, go and pick up Lili from home to give her a ride to a friend's house and go to pick up Yasmin. In the middle of this whole chaos, I also had to prepare dinner and clean up.

I don't know what I'm doing anymore! Seriously, I feel more and more like I'm burning the candle at both ends. I'm not sure if I should have gone back to work or even gotten married. I know it's a weird thing to say, especially when I look at my beautiful children! I'm truly blessed with them, and I couldn't imagine my life without them. A single person would probably tell me that working is my own decision and a single working mom would tell me that I should be happy that I have no bills to pay on top of everything else. It's a weird, weird situation.

And the truce sign with Amir only held this long. I was so tired when he got home that we ended up screaming and yelling at each other again. I have no idea why this man has such a traditional mindset. I mean if I didn't know him better, I would think that he's a Taliban! Seriously! I can't even believe what I'm writing: He told me that I should be a good mother and wife by just staying home! I asked him why he hadn't told me this when we met because I would never have gotten married to such a backward-thinking man. He answered that I exaggerate how bad my situation is and that

I'm always nagging about everything. He compared it to me saying that I'm starving at a fully set table. Blah, blah, blah!

Maybe I shouldn't have stayed home when the girls were young to get Amir used to the idea of a working mother. His mom was always home, and maybe he's just used to the picture of a 1950s apron-wearing smiling mom. He would love to have one of those, who regardless of whether she works or not, still has on full makeup; welcomes him at the door in black lingerie and high heels; and says with a very sexy, smoky voice, "Here's your martini, darling!" You know, I would love to be more seductive, but after working seven hours a day and then being my children's chauffeur, in-home tutor, cook, and maid, I simply don't have the energy of being a bombshell in person.

I think, with all due respect to men, they still need to get used to today's woman. Maybe they'll get used to them by the time their own daughters are in my situation. You always see things differently when your own child is involved. I remember my mom told me once that my father had some disagreements with my grandfather and now my father has the same disagreements with his son-in-law.

I swear I was never a typical conflict-avoiding girl, but I wasn't a streetfighter-type either. I like some arguments because it makes your brain work. On the other hand, my brain must be burned out from all the debates and lung exercises of the past few years.

Sometimes I think the arranged marriages of the past were maybe better. At least those people only had expectations, and no feelings, involved. I think we all tend to have a certain picture of our loved one and get so easily disappointed when it doesn't turn out to be true. Love shouldn't have anything to do with expectations and still it makes us believe in a fairy tale.

I remember when I was Lili's age and I was still living in France. I had this very bad crush on Jean-Paul, a boy who happened to look like James Dean and also completely ignored me. I could have dropped dead in front of him, and he would have only stepped over my corpse. I was so desperately in love with him that I thought I would die if I couldn't be with him. Well, one day I got up all my courage and called him, just to hear his voice. My whole heart was trembling. And unfortunately I still remember every word he said.

He told me, "You're too young for me. Do you think I'm stupid enough to go out with you?"

"Yes," I replied with a shaky voice.

☺

"Call me when you're of legal age!" he snapped and then quickly hung up on me.

(Oh my gosh, I can't believe that that was so long ago.) I was devastated! I had been hoping to be recognized by him and finally hear his voice, but I was crushed after a four-minute phone conversation.

And that's exactly my point! Why was I devastated? Because I felt something for him. If I hadn't felt anything and he reacted the way he did, I would have only said, "Kiss my bony ass!" I wouldn't even think about him anymore.

Many years later a friend of mine actually told me that back then Jean-Paul had had a crush on a girl, who didn't like him at all. There's my point again. He had been reaching for a girl he couldn't have.

I guess when people who are madly in love get married, the same thing happens: You realize that the person is different; you have heartache. If you didn't care about him or her, you wouldn't care too much about the relationship because it would be just like the mutual agreements of arranged marriages in the past. Back then the women would get financial security, and the men would get boys to carry on the family name and warm meals for dinner.

Look at our lives now! Either while working or studying, both men and women are seeking financially independence and a career. No one cares too much about male offspring or warm meals. The sexes need each other even less now.

Anja told me the other day that she sees guys as potential good sperm banks for her future kids. She doesn't want anything more. I thought that I was liberal. Beat that.

To get back to my first point, early on Amir and I never fought as much about gender equality, or as he likes to call it "women's penis-growing stage." (I hate it when he makes fun of my gender.

But again, before saying good night, I changed the subject, just so that we wouldn't go to sleep right after fighting. Even though we sleep in different beds. I guess this harmony-loving creature of my grandmother's time is still somewhere deep in me.

Go figure.

June 26, 2006

I have had coffee nearly every other day with Steven! And today it happened!!! He kissed me!

We were walking down the street to my office building and he took my hand while walking next to me. *Nice!* I thought. My hand felt great being in his. Right before we were standing in front of the office building, he walked me into an empty drive way, leaned over and kissed me. Not long, not too wet, but a passionate kiss. Felt wonderful!

June 27, 2006

Today was last day of school. Finally! With all the snow days we had during the past winter, the school year ended so late. Much later than usual. The last day of course means tons of teachers' gifts, which I still don't get because the year is over, meaning you can't bribe the teachers anymore.

This afternoon I explained to Lili and Yasmin that I wouldn't fly with them to France to see my parents but would come later. This was a disaster.

"But you always come with us," one moaned.

"Your work is so much more important to you than your kids," the other noted with a pout.

There were countless whys. I guess they're still younger than I assume. They look so much more mature, wearing makeup and Victoria's Secret pushup bras, that I assume their brains are growing at the same rate as their boobs. I guess I should compare most girls, including mine, to little girls playing dress-up. I tried to explain to them that due to their father's and my decision to—most likely—get a divorce, I needed to save some money. Then I tried explaining that I had just started a new job and couldn't go on a vacation so quickly after starting. I would try to come to France at a later time.

I tried to make them happier by buying them summer stuff for vacation, and it worked for the moment. We had dinner at their favorite restaurant, and finally by the end of the night, they were doing somewhat better.

July 13, 2006

I haven't had an e-mail from Steven in nearly five days now. I wonder what's going on with him. Then he called this afternoon, on my way home, but he sounded in a rush. He wanted to cancel our dinner tonight. I asked him if everything was okay, and he became very unfriendly.

"You've started to behave like a typical woman," he snapped.

Ah, hello, I'm one!

"You don't have to tell me about every detail of your day," I replied.

I really did not know what to say because I actually never asked him about every step of his day. *Aren't you the one calling and e-mailing me all the time?* I thought.

Then he started his usual sweet talk, but it just sounded like a recording to me. As I listened, I noticed some strange things. He barely says my name. Usually he calls me "honey" or "baby." *Ah,* I thought. *It probably is his line, and to save his fat ass, he calls all of his ladies the same sweet nicknames to not mix up their names.*

Another thing is he never asks about the specifics of my work or personal life. When we first started talking, I told him about my work and some small daily issues, but he never followed up about them. What I thought was male disinterest and forgetfulness now came across as ignorance. I know, men usually don't overanalyze like women. Their memories are less intertwined, and they don't see the difference between two pairs of black shoes. But if a man is really, truly interested in a woman, wouldn't he at least once in a while ask, "Oh, yeah, I remember you told me about this. How's going?"? He never does.

I wouldn't be a woman if I can't find out what's going on. I just have to figure out how. I will let him sweet-talk me some more until I have a plan. Ha!

This is getting good. Ha ha!

July 17, 2006

Steven is somehow too good to be true. I just have the crazy feeling that he would sweet-talk any woman, so I had this devilish plan of inventing a gorgeous woman and putting her profile on the job network, just to see if he hits on her. I mean, I really shouldn't trust a man I have only seen for a couple of times, right? I'm over the age of dating here and there and being made a fool in front of—not only the guy—but my girls also.

I named the profile Giselle, took a picture of some unknown model, and sent him a contact request. I pretended that she had some money to invest. Ha ha ha! He immediately accepted and then I let one thing lead to another, and she asked him whether they could meet. He immediately told her that he thought she was very, very attractive, and he would love to meet her—after barely five hours!

I just couldn't believe it! I mean, he was literally meeting me behind my own back!

Then he constantly told me that fucking nonsense that he was *so* extremely busy. When a guy works a lot from the very beginning and he says that he's busy, he's telling you the truth. But if he's being Mr. Casanova at the beginning and then all of a sudden he becomes Mr. Busy-Busy, something is wrong.

Well, anyway, I let Giselle be the sexiest girl, a man's dream come true. She sent Steven some lingerie and bikini pictures of herself from her newly created e-mail account. Meanwhile he told me, that some crazy girl (aka Giselle,) had requested to be networked with him, and he felt so weird about it. It was all bullshit because he had set a date with her at his office to go over some investment questions she had and that she was interested to have him as a personal realtor, but he was lying straight to my face because the appointment was at a fancy restaurant.

Can you just imagine me at my computer? My blood was boiling with anger, and then I was cooking up sweet revenge. Once I started laughing hilariously, and then I started sobbing like a maniac. It was so sad.

This guy who I thought was my friend was cheating on me with myself. I know it's not technically cheating, but it still confirmed that he was just too good to be true. He isn't trustworthy.

I'll continue this game just to see how far he would go. Maybe I'm too harsh; maybe he won't even meet with her or maybe he'll mention that he's already seeing someone. We'll see.

July 18, 2006

Well, he hasn't told her anything yet, but the funny thing is that all of a sudden he has tons of time—*for her*. He sends me an e-mail and moans on the phone that he's so extremely busy while he types e-mails to her all the time.

I told Lili and Yasmin about it, and they laugh when I tell them that I'm jealous of myself. But honestly, I'm also having my fun mostly because I came to the conclusion that I'm just too damn stupid when it comes to men!

Most people talk about a gut feeling you get when you think something isn't right in a relationship, and it's true. I had a weird feeling when I saw him for the first time and spoke to him. But because of how I'm wired, I had to see if he was nice. But not my gut tells me something is up, and if you don't feel right, it's simply not worth it. Don't even try to play games with your feelings.

I love to blame my parents for the way I act toward men. In reality it's probably partially them and mostly me. I can't always blame someone else; it's just more convenient.

You know, I've learned so much in my life, which just goes with the territory. I learned to knit, sew, speak foreign languages, drive, ride a bike, fly an airplane, and do all the things, but no one ever taught me about two things: how to be wife and a parent. These are the things life gives you, and it has to be difficult and you have to do the wrong thing sometimes because that's how you really learn.

But what if I don't want to make mistakes? What if I don't want to stand there like a fool for once? Huh? What then? With Amir I thought, H*e was the one; he's the man, who makes me happy. He's a good Persian boy from a good*

Persian family. That will keep my parents happy. But he grew up in the West, just like me, so he'll understand me.

Look, I know I'm not making sense because this has nothing to do with Steven directly. But I promise you it does! I mean, don't you see that I'm always making the same mistake over and over again? First, my mistake is called Amir and then it's Steven. It's the same mistake, just with a different name. They have the same common denominator: They're men. I just never learned how to handle them: I believe everything they say. Sure, there are some men who don't fall into the bad-boy category—and probably they aren't bad men—but I'm just attracted to one type of guy. With Steven, I was just smarter by inventing Giselle to see what a lying slimeball he is. The funny thing is while he was sending e-mails to Giselle and me, I had to re-invent myself as Giselle and revert back to me as I responded to him, which was clever.

Maybe I should be proud of that instead of accusing my parents of not teaching me how to deal with men, bashing men, or, even worse, looking down on myself.

July 19, 2006

Giselle decided to meet with Steven, which he then told me, but he left out one major part: He said that he wanted to show her an apartment she had shown interest in. *Apartment, my ass,* I thought. *He just probably wants to fuck her on the floor of that place. He had told her to put on the outfit from one of the pictures, because it was sexually stimulating! He wrote her even which shoes to wear and what he likes the most! Then he comes back to me and pretends to be the oh-so sweet one.* He does not know that I am Giselle and he talks only about sex with her. Which of course Giselle enjoys. Let's say it this way. Giselle's responses would make a Penthouse editor blush. And of course Steven keeps saying that he can't wait to see her and do her. All I can say is: Wow! That's called speedy! Waists no time if he has the opportunity. I assume the only reason he did not talk to me about sex is because I didn't initiate it. Instead I spoke about everything except sex.

Why on earth would Steven even tell me about her anyway? It's not as if he's having a relationship with her or is he? On the other hand, he does not have a relation-ship with me either. I mean we kissed, but I would not call it a steady relation-ship yet. It might have been going towards it, but wasn't there yet. I'm not cheating, that's for sure. Amir and I are just sharing the house, but there's no relationship there.

This dilemma has been on my mind before: When does cheating start? Are you cheating when you're chatting with someone on Facebook? Or when you're e-mailing them? Or is it when you look at someone's naked picture and get excited?

And for whom? Can it be called cheating if you're still legally married, aren't together, but are living in the same house? I think it should be called *cheating* when you pretend to be happily married or in a relationship and your spouse or significant other believes everything is okay, but you're fantasizing about someone else.

But that in a way that needs to be clarified as well. What if a guy watched a movie with a big-boobed porn star and he pretends he's doing her? I wouldn't call that *cheating*. He doesn't "connect" with the woman on the screen. She's just a "jump" starter—to get him going so he can go and have sex with his wife or girlfriend.

At my last office, a girl had seen her husband downloading porn on his computer at home, and she was so upset.

"Why?" I asked.

"He's cheating on me," she replied.

"Did he touch any of them? Did he sleep with them or tell them that he loved them?" I asked. "No, so just relax."

But that might be too liberal.

Well anyway, to get back to my main story. Obviously Giselle never showed up because she doesn't exist. I thought about "dumping" Steven—maybe dumping's not be the right word because I don't think we had a serious relation-ship. We never openly committed to each other. I'll basically ignore him. We'll see if he gets the message.

July 27, 2006

Who said I couldn't ignore the man?

Steven called and wanted to give me his usual useless sweet-talk speech. I told him that I was so busy that I couldn't talk to him. He sent me text after text and followed them up with e-mails. But honestly, the reason why I didn't answer him wasn't because he's an idiot. It's simply because I realized how much of an idiot I had been.

I was telling Lili and Yasmin about what life was like as a woman. I told them that they should learn from my mistakes and feel free to make their own in life. I know I have a very open relationship with my girls, but some moms don't. I feel bad for those mothers. Some moms pretend that they're holy and have never done anything wrong. That's not me.

I like my girls to be involved in my life and see the struggles and rewards I've endured. I told them that they shouldn't necessarily look for someone to complete them. I think that's what my invention of Giselle taught me. It's like I feel that I have to have a man on my side. I know that sounds weird when I say that because I'm a liberated woman, or as Amir once called me "a wisecracking and man-castrating bitch." Wow!

Why am I always trying to look for this acceptance from a man? I wish I knew the answer to that question—or maybe I do. I think most women do, but women of my generation aren't used to their positions in society. Our mothers fought for equality. They were the ones who burned their bras, fought for access to the birth-control pill, and said, "Screw men! We don't want to live under their rules, and we can do anything we want." That part was awesome. But they gave us, their daughters, the burden of living in that freedom. They expected us to live, for them, the life for which they had fought. I heard this sentiment often from my mom and the mothers of my friends: "Do this! Do that! We had to fight for it!" I never knew why I had to do everything a man does. I liked to challenge boys, even at a young age. I liked running faster and climbing higher, and it would have fine if that princess that's inside of every little girl hadn't existed.

See our mothers were forced to behave like that little princess, so they tore off their tiaras. I saw pictures of my mom and her friends at my age, and I was struck by their femininity. I wondered about myself as I stared at the photos: *Why are they the ones bashing femininity when they were so feminine and beautiful?* You see I had been born as part of a mission: Be like a man, think like a man, and look like a lady. Does that make sense?

Lili and Yasmin have no idea how privileged they are. Their generation has the rights, and they have a choice. They simply grow up with the idea of emancipation without being forced to live up to a certain image. They're aware of their femininity; they're okay with showing off their bras, which my mother's generation forcefully burned; they're okay with a boy hugging them or seeing them as a female object. I guess, my generation was in the middle of the two "normal" generations. The older generation made it easy for the younger generation, and my generation was just used as an umbilical cord.

I look at my grandmother, who was completely dependant on her husband financially, and in a way she seemed happier.

Enh, I'm not sure where emancipation got us. We're fighting to be like men, and when they treat us like one of them, we get insulted. If a guy opens the door for you, you say, "Idiot, I can do it myself." But when he doesn't, we say,

"What an ass! He didn't even open the door for me." That's the internal battle between being the princess and the you-can-piss-while-standing girl. We are stuck in the middle.

As for Steven, I think I'm going to leave that chapter. I'm done with it—no man for a while.

August 15, 2006

So, what's new except being very busy at work? Let me think. It's vacation time. The girls are in France after attending a couple of camps. I met a couple of very nice ladies at different occasions. Amir is—well—Amir.

I bought some very sexy clothes for the summer and have had fun wearing them. I'm trying to get a tan. I heard that applying olive oil to your skin before sunbathing works, but I haven't tried it yet because I really don't want to smell like a garden salad. Hey, if I run out of perfume, I should try it.

I'm still wondering why women have to shave their legs in the summertime. Okay, we don't have to, but I would love to see the male look be in style, mostly because guys always ask why women take so long to get ready and can't shower in five seconds. Well, first we have to shave all the hair from places, where we didn't even know that hair would grow, then we need full-body loofah scrub, then we have to coat ourselves in shower lotion, and finally after a normal shampoo, we have to condition and sometimes use a hair mask on our hair. That's just in the shower. After we get out it's foot cream, body cream, hand cream, under-eye lotion, and moisturizer for the rest of the face. At that point we might be done. ☺

There are other unspoken rules as well. We can never dry our feet with the same towel as we use on our faces. I guess that's worse than smelling like a salad. What's next? Okay we can't let our hair air-dry—unless you want to have a straight curtain or an afro look. That calls for curling cream or straightening cream before we attack our hair with heat.

I know it's oh-so complicated, but guess what, men? Suck it up and live with it! A lady never takes a shower in five minutes by just standing under the warm stream of water—unless you want to see us as nature intended. I'm just not sure miniskirts and shorts with hairy legs would be an enjoyable sight. Ha ha.

Yeah, it would be nice to have at least an hour for the described regimen above, but reality limits it five to ten minutes. It doesn't require an astrophysicist to achieve, just a much more complex female brain.

Okay, so back to the summer, what else have I done? I read a couple of good books. Now with the kids gone for most of the summer, it's easier to read at night.

The funny thing is I usually don't see Amir, but if I do, we're somewhat civilized. I wonder why people say that when you don't get along well, you should have children to straighten things up. I think it's actually quite the opposite. No marriage works and increases the bonding when you have kids. With kids all you notice are the differences. Why? Personalities don't change, and as you try to raise your kiddos, your personalities appear much more on the surface, bringing up every different understanding each of you has about that very important task. It's kind of like a team where the members don't click. Maybe the idea of having kids to fix a marriage was for ancient times when women didn't have anything to do until they had babies. Now that we want to share the responsibility, which is how it should be, we should put that idea to rest. Or maybe we should just reproduced without males. Who needs the famous multitasking tool?

Oh, I guess I lost myself on a different topic again.

Okay, so I had requested five days off when I was hired and will take off next week to see the girls in France. I'm so excited! I can't wait to see the girls and my parents.

I also will get together my friends from school. It's always so funny when we get together. Although we are all moms and dads now, we still behave like ten-year-olds when we have these casual reunions. Many things are so predictable: Emma turned out to be a lesbian—I always knew it, Lia has her fifth baby, and Barb got her second divorce. Wow, that sounds awful, doesn't it? Each one of our lives has gone down a somewhat obvious path. I guess we all start with a set of cards, and it depends how you play them, order in which you lay them on the table.

I remember when we were twelve and had just found about some magazines that would answer all of our sexual questions. It still cracks us up when we talk about it.

Okay, that's enough for now. I have to do some laundry and clean the bathrooms.

August 26, 2006

So I met another guy. I know my diary sounds like a checklist of men by now. I have no idea how these guys suddenly start falling into my life like raindrops. I have known this guy, Paul, for some time. By *known*, I don't mean "known-known" but "seen-known." His daughter is in the same grade as Yasmin. I saw him, smiling at me, in another line at the grocery store. I smiled back, and one smile led to another. I could tell he recognized me as well, and we started chatting with the usual small talk. He told me that he had been divorced for four years now, and I told him that I was in the process of filing.

"I can help you make the right decisions as you move forward," he told me.

Yeah right, I thought. *You just want to* help *me.*

Well, we decided to meet for coffee on the weekend. The girls will be in Europe, so I might as well keep myself busy.

After coming home, I wasn't too sure if I should actually go out with that guy. I remembered what Annie, a friend of mine, told me at a lunch before she moved to Florida a few years ago, "He used to cheat on his wife all the time."

But hey, it's just a coffee, right? Nothing serious, I mean I'm still "legally"—a funny term—married to Amir. I just want to have someone to occasionally go out with or have dinner with when the girls aren't around. It's not anything serious. That's not bad, is it?

At times, I think about all the people I've met in my life. What would have happened if I had made different decisions at certain times? Like in my marriage to Amir?

It's like shopping for clothes. When you have a party to go to, the first question in your head is, *What shall I wear?* I usually imagine myself at that certain event wearing the different choices. You should try to do this with certain men. It's interesting. You ask yourself, *What would have happened?* It becomes a whole story, and you imagine yourself with a different spouse, family, and lifestyle.

It's too bad that with men, unlike the outfit example, you can't change your mind after trying them on for five seconds. When you don't want to wear something, you simply don't. You keep the receipt and return it. A return policy is much tougher between two people.

August 30, 2006

The girls will return from France this evening, just in time for school tomorrow. Not sure why I always listen to them and book their flights for the last day. I had just returned home when I received a text from Paul, asking me if I wanted to have dinner with him tonight. *Okay, coffee becomes dinner,* I thought. *That's not bad.* I suggested several places, and he said they were all good, but he mentioned that he was a fabulous cook and wanted to make me dinner.

I don't know why I didn't think about Amir.

"Fine," I said. "Let's have dinner at your place."

On my way to his home, it occurred to me that I really didn't know much about him. *Actually, I don't know him at all,* I thought. *I hope he's not a crazy guy.*

Well, his house was very neat and well decorated. It was manly, but hey, he's a man. His dinner was good: some grilled vegetable, roasted chicken, and some salad. We talked about everything: the past, the present, and the future. No, it wasn't about a future as in *our* future, but generally in regard to our kids and life as single parents. He told me a little bit about his divorce and how tough it was for him. I never thought of him as emotional, but I guess some men suffer more than others if their marriages don't work out. (I don't think that Amir will be one of them, but probably my brother, Sam, probably would.)

At the end of the night, he walked me to my car and hugged me. There was no kissing or anything. He was very much a gentleman.

Then I drove to the airport to pick up my girls! So excited to see them and hear all their summer adventures and listen to their voices filling each room with laughter! My babies! ☺

August 31, 2006

The kids' school started today. Summer is over and too bad I could not join the girls in France. I would have not only loved to see my parents and my old friends, but also get a break from this life here. Sitting in a café in the morning with a chocolate croissant and a café au lait. Enjoying the people, the language, the air, the parks and walking from store to store, since finding a parking spot would take more than hours. Well… I'm exaggerating of course. Not hours, but when you found one empty spot, you are more than happy to leave your car there and walk for the rest of the time. It is not a cliché; life is always different in the place you grew up. That place embraces you and hold you as if you were still a child. Oh well. Here it's back to normal life—well, as normal as life gets around here. It's funny how I have two kids and feel overwhelmed at times. My grandmother had six children and was the most relaxed person. She told me once that I definitely had more work with my two than she would have ever been able to accept. She had nannies for each child; she didn't drive, cook, clean, or do laundry. But when you ask her children if she was and is a good mother, there's no hesitation before they say, "Yes!"

There's that generational difference again. I was unemployed and was unhappy; now I'm employed and even though I love the job, I'm still not happy. What is it with me or any other career woman? Maybe we're overbooked?

I went online and started searching for "what makes working women happy." The answers ranged from certain spa procedures to certain sex positions to one specific entry, "Be a woman." *Okay,* I thought. *The last time I checked, I hadn't grown balls, but I'll work on seeing how else I can keep my gender intact.*

I also found a couple of miracle-promising face lotions in my search. Based on the description of this product, I could put it on my great-grandmother's face at night—she might have the face of a plissé skirt—and voilà, she would wake up with the face of an eighteen-year-old. Do the cosmetic companies actually think that we believe in that crap? I mean, come on, getting wrinkles is part of the natural skin process, right? I admit I have some small ones around my eyes, but I actually never thought much about them until I read that article. *Great!* I thought. *Now I have to run and get that lotion because I now know that I don't look like eighteen anymore.*

Why is it that as a woman I always think that the more expensive the lotion, the better it must work. I remember my great-aunt, who had never heard of the fancy brand names, only put some moisturizer on her face and made sure she avoided the sun. Oh man, she looked good. Yeah, yeah, I know it also has to do with genes. But hey, the best lotion and the best genes won't help if you worry constantly, don't get enough sleep, and don't eat right.

I ran to my mirror, the one that magnifies fifteen times. Okay, I have some rosacea and I missed a hair on my upper lip when I waxed, but otherwise I was pleased.

In the end great skin is a combination of all factors, not just the hole in your pocketbook from purchasing miracle cream. Maybe you can't buy happiness after all.

September 11, 2006

I remember this day five years ago; it was the turning point in my religious belief. Until then, I had no idea about the religion into which I was born. In many Persian families, we had religion but never thought about how others perceived it. I was brought up with believing that my religion was about believing in peace and equality—but most of all, it was very private. When I say "turning point," I mean that I realized that some people would rather force their belief on others.

Both sides of a fight usually hold to some reasonable opinions. But I still don't know. I try to understand why people would publicly use something so private and something that should bring peace is a weapon to kill.

I knew some people who were physically killed on that day, but also some people who mentally injured in the aftermath, never being able to forget those images—on many parts of the globe. It's all so wrong, but mostly so sad. May all the innocent people who lost their lives that day rest in peace.

September 16, 2007

Just tell me one thing: If Yasmin's dance recital is in December, why on earth do they already have rehearsals in mid-September? The woman sent me the rehearsal schedule for the next four months—with a practice nearly every day. I know it must be tough hopping around onstage. (And yes, I wouldn't be able to do this; well actually I would, but it would be comedic.)

I know that Lili will explode when I tell her because I'll be hauling Yasmin back and forth and Lili might have to skip a couple of her lacrosse games.

I guess the dance instructors don't realize that people have several kids, work, and a home. And I absolutely refuse to be one of those mothers who feeds her kids a sandwich in the car and says, "Honey, just don't spill anything on your math homework." On second thought maybe I should become like that. Maybe my life is like this, just because I refused to compromise and tried to do everything.

Yesterday when I was at Amy's house for lunch, we were talking about this exact dilemma. She only has one child, Mattie.

"Most of our dinners end up being in the car," she confessed to me. "I don't think Mattie has done her homework at a desk for more than a year now."

And Amy isn't even working! Well, she does, but it's only two hours a day at the library.

And look at me, I thought as I listened to her. *I'm working fulltime, have two kids, clean my home, still iron my clothes, and try to cook every night.*

"I think women are burning the candle on both ends," I explained. "At work, we think of our families and feel bad that we aren't at school, helping with every little volunteer job. When we're with our family, we constantly think about all the unfinished projects at work."

She listened and nodded. "But there's nothing we can do about it."

"I disagree," I replied. "I think we can do something. We can't simply sit back and think that society has given us these roles or that it's men's fault. Blaming others is just too easy. It's a situation we were born into. We have to make it clear to everyone from the very beginning that we are two-headed people. We have a double existence." I know admitting this does not address the problem. Instead, we have to find a solution. But what?

As we kept chatting, I thought about how I had gotten into this double life. I hate regret because I always think that at the time I made the decision I thought it was best, but if I could go back, I would have done things a lot differently. I would have said after Yasmin was born that I wanted to go back to work—even if it was just a part-time job—instead of sitting at home seven years and raising my kids. It would have forced me out of the house. The change wouldn't have been so drastic for Amir. He would have gotten used to my working outside the house as well.

At work, I would have mentioned from the beginning that I needed "mother-friendly hours," instead of saying "yes" and "amen" to everything they said. I wouldn't have been so desperate for work and so happy that I had found a job that I would agree to everything without setting conditions.

At home after I had had Lili and Yasmin, I couldn't believe that I was a mother, so I tried to enjoy every second. I didn't think that my precious babies would grow into young ladies one day who were quite happy without my following them the whole day. I shouldn't have devoted myself completely to my family because in the end I'm left alone. My girls will say, "Thank you," but they'll also say, "We didn't force you to stay home." I think it's much better for them to see that their mother is a fighter and that she didn't lose her existence. (Also, most men—Amir is the exception—have much more respect for women who have a certain degree of financial independence.)

I think I'll remind my girls of these things when they grow up. But in the end, Lili and Yasmin will make their own mistakes and learn from them.

It's also cowardly for me to continue to blame my mother's generation. The women of the 1960s and 1970s were fighting to break out, and my generation ended up with this freedom without being told how to use it—because no one knew how. My girls' generation will be used to this freedom. They'll be free to stay home or work, and I think their generation will be less judgmental toward each other.

Otherwise, the lunch was nice and very relaxing. I told Amy that we should do it more often—of course if time allows.

Okay, I still have to clean up the family room, and tomorrow is another day of work.

September 19, 2007

I have this weird feeling again about Paul. He seems so absent minded. During our conversations, he constantly checks his phone to see whether he got messages, randomly gets up to go to the bathroom and takes his phone with him, and is weird. It was the same feeling I had about Steven. So I decided to allow another visit from my man-seducing woman, our friend *Giselle*.

She entered the scene and—bam, Paul has all this time all of a sudden. *For her.* It's Steven all over again

I'm getting used to inventing this type of girl. Isn't it funny that I started getting out of my own relationship with Amir and tried to get to know some men, but in the end I'm getting to know myself. Maybe it means something that I'm inventing this completely different woman and feel so good playing her? Maybe something deep inside of me still wants to be an actress and play different parts? Or maybe every woman is a sum of a Giselle, me, and other female characters? In the end we eventually play all of these expected roles throughout the day, don't we?

So Giselle has entered the scene, and Paul sure fell for her. The worst thing is that the idiot didn't even notice that she kept asking him about every one of his female friends. Maybe he didn't notice because Giselle tends to be very sexual and very graphic about her sexual tastes. He was distracted.

Oh, Paul, you're such an idiot, I thought, *so much so that you have no idea. This is just the beginning. Wait until Giselle asks you about me!*

September 20, 2006

So Giselle asked him about me—of course not directly. That would have been weird. Ha ha. She worked herself into the direction, by asking questions like "So, what did you do last night?" Basically, she was digging for information about his activities anytime I was with him. (At least he doesn't play electronic ping-pong by e-mailing Giselle [meaning me] and then me.)

He said, "Yeah, last night I was watching a movie with a friend."

"A normal friend or a sex friend or a more serious friend?" Giselle asked.

"Normal friend," he replied.

I thought, *Okay, at least that's nice; he doesn't plan of getting me into his bed right now.*

Giselle and Paul kept going back and forth about me, but then the chatter abruptly stopped when he said, "She's too serious. I think she wants to try to make me start a relationship with her."

I nearly fell from my chair. When exactly did I give an indication of anything like that? I guess men interpret questions as questioning and don't see it as pure curiosity. He was clearly making this up. Giselle had to know more.

"What ever do you mean, Paul?"

Paul replied with tons of stories, saying that I had some issues, I didn't know what I wanted, and more nonsense like that.

"I told her that she was highstrung and then immediately started talking with her about sex," he continued.

Really?!?! I thought. *I don't remember that.*

While I was fuming on the inside, I had to keep my cool, so that he wouldn't realize Giselle was me. I kept the electronic conversation going for a few more minutes before signing off. Just like that, Giselle was gone.

The whole chat made me really sad.

Why do men always think that we immediately want to get married? Even if they're pretending to be interested in a relationship, they really don't want one. Sally, a coworker at my former job, had been on a dating Web site, and she mentioned that ninety-eight percent of those guys, even if they said on their profiles that they were looking for a serious relationship, just wanted a sex.

"One of the guys asked me within three e-mails what my favorite position was in bed," she told me.

I thought, *Come on! Are you serious?*

At least wait until the fourth e-mail—ha ha!

Anyway back to Paul, now that I know what he really thinks of me, I know how to act as *me*.

September 21, 2006

So here's the dilemma for the day: On my way to work, I received a call from Diane. She was all nervous and seemed as if she had been crying for a while. Of course, I was worried, and after asking her what was going on, she blurted out, "I'm pregnant." Usually I would scream of joy, but I could sense that something wasn't right, so I didn't congratulate her.

Instead I asked, "And?"

She and her boyfriend are both healthy, they have a good income, and it seems like a good relationship. Something had to be wrong for her not to be happy.

"It wasn't planned, and I haven't told Brian yet."

Hmm, I thought. I told her to calm down and asked her meet me for coffee.

An hour and a half later, I had the entire story. Apparently, Brian comes from a family where everyone gets married first and then starts a family. Plus, his family isn't too fond of Diane because she breaks from these traditional ideas and has mentioned at several events that she isn't a very religious person. I had no idea about all of this.

"What are you planning to do?" I asked her.

"I'm thinking about having an abortion," she answered.

I was somewhat surprised.

"Why not adoption or try raising the child yourself?" I countered.

"I've thought about all the options. I just wonder if an abortion would best. Then I can forget that this ever happened."

I was lost. What do you say to a woman who is expecting a child? Don't get me wrong. But it's not my decision even though I want to help her.

It occupied my mind the entire day. Here we have mostly men, sitting in Congress and deciding what the options are for pregnant women, and here I am, a woman, who has had two pregnancies and doesn't have an answer. It made me realize that regardless of all the liberty we have, we still aren't hundred percent free to decide about our own bodies. (And yes, there are women who are against abortions and men who say the laws should be pro-choice.)

It should be every woman's right to decide what she wants to do with her pregnancy. Don't give me those arguments that as soon as the sperm hits the egg, it's a living creature and abortion would be killing someone. If that's the case, I would ask, "What about all the eggs that depart a woman's body during menstruation? What about all the sperm that aren't used? Even though they are two independent elements and don't create a baby by themselves. Is that killing half of what is necessary to make a baby? Is a woman killing a baby when she uses an IUD?"

Let's examine the issue from all angles. Does anyone know what a woman goes through when she decides to have an abortion? Does anyone believe that a woman just gets pregnant and has an abortion for fun? That it's like having a chat about buying the latest fashion, "Oh, I haven't had an abortion yet, but so-and-so did. I feel so left out." Do these guys actually understand that the entire hormonal system of a woman's body changes? Do they know that a woman usually notices within a couple of hours after conception that something is different? Those men better; otherwise how dare they decide what a woman should do? How dare they say that a woman is killing a human being if they don't even know how it feels to be pregnant? Do they know that usually after the first ultrasound the gynecologist tells them the approximate birthday and that the woman who has an abortion might think of that date for years to come? I don't think so.

Look at it if the roles were reversed. Do I decide if men should take pills to increase their penis size or increase their sperm count? Ha, I would love to see some the women in Congress vote on that!

The fact is that it should be every woman's personal decision.

Okay, I'll give it a twist. It's her decision as long as it's medically safe and the fetus wouldn't be deemed a child yet (basically as soon as it can live outside the mother's womb).

I always think about what will happen to that "unplanned" or "unwanted" child. Do these men decide about their future as well? Are they saving money to send that child to school and make sure that he or she grows up in a safe environment? Isn't it better to not bring a baby into this world if you can't take care of him or her?

We talk constantly about decreasing criminal activity through increasing taxes to have youth centers and other programs. Did it ever occur to someone to ask all the kids who have been in trouble why they act the way they so? I'm not saying that every criminal adolescent should have been aborted, but what I'm saying is that it should be the mother who decides if she'll have the means to raise that child in a safe environment.

That night I called Diane.

"Whatever decision you make has to come from you," I counseled her. "No one should or can take that away from you, and no one should try to influence you."

"Thanks," she replied. "That's the best advice anyone has ever given me. I know it's a tough decision, but it will be one I have to live with for the rest of my life."

September 23, 2006

One of the women at work decided to move. What I heard was that she had a big house and now wanted to downsize to a condo. At lunch she told us how difficult it was to get rid of things to fit everything into the smaller place.

That's probably true, I thought. What would bother me the most would be choosing what should go into what pile: the "I don't-need-this-but-I'm-oh-so-good-by-donating-it" pile, the "throw-it-away-immediately-because-I-can't-believe-I-have-this" pile, and the "awww-do-you-remember" pile, which is the hardest to part with.

She said that she threw out a huge container of stuff. Then she looked at things from her grown-up kids and asked them to decide what they wanted to keep. *Wow,* I thought. *I mean, you have to have time for that. If I ever asked my kids what they want to keep; we would end up in a war zone.* Lili would probably throw out all the things that make me sentimental because she claims to hate "antiques," which means she hates anything that is older than a month. Yasmin would be amazed that she even had all this stuff. I can hear her saying, "What is this? I didn't know I had that."

Even though I always say that I would love to move, I'm not sure I ever could. There are so many memories connected to every corner. But on the other hand, I think that in moments of separation from anyone or anything, we see the good moments only, instead of the objective situation. That's good when you are saying good-bye to people because you suddenly realize what a person actually meant to you and you feel awful that you didn't appreciate every second with him or her. But that doesn't happen with objects. Or is a house filled with memories not an object because it's filled with those memories? I mean, if I remove every personal effect from the house, can I still say that I miss it? Isn't it the memory in my head, which most likely changes with time, that I actually miss?

(My dad always says that you should enjoy that very moment, that breath, because it will never come back. Even if you could physically go back to that moment, guess what? It won't be the same again.)

Back to my coworker, she said that it's so tough to be at work and moving at the same time because she will have no idea where the movers put each box. You figure that they would put a box labeled *bathroom* in the bathroom and not in the kitchen, right? Oh well. She also said as soon as she gets settled—in about a week or so—she would like to invite us all over for coffee. I'm looking forward to it. I'm so blessed to have this job and no bitchy Liz anymore. Yeah!

September 25, 2006

Why do all the guys I meet start off as princes and end up as frogs? I mean, come on! Is it so difficult to find someone who's somewhat decent looking and has some brains? Oh, and honesty should be part of the deal, too.

The latest guy, Paul, is such a big talker. I guess he stands in front of the mirror and just makes up this philosophical shit. He thinks he knows oh so much. Bullshit. He needs a shrink. He tells me he slept with more than 150 women in a year, and now he is trying to analyze me. *Shut up!* I thought as he went on. *I mean, "Fuck you!" Who are you to come by and try to save me now? I mean what gives you the balls to come into my life, tell me all this nonsense sweet talk, kiss me tenderly, and, within three weeks, try to analyze me and tell me that you want to mentor me in life? Go screw yourself.* I've never been so mad in my life. At least I have some decency to fake interest for a little longer.

He called me earlier today and asked whether I wanted to have some dinner with him. "Fine," I said. *Now that I know what he thinks of me, I'll pay him back and at least have some fun,* I thought to myself. I'll remind you that I have no interest in him whatsoever.

At dinner he tried to tell me that I was uptight because of my Persian upbringing. That was it. I had had it.

"Screw you," I snapped. "Maybe I'm uptight because of guys like you. Maybe it's because I'm sick and tired of being told how good-looking I am—just to try to land me in your fucking bed. Maybe for me it's more important that a man can keep his testosterone in control and stop trying to play my daddy. I'm so sick of men who are guided from the waist down. I just want to have a normal conversation. What's wrong with that? Is it a problem that I prefer to talk about the economy more than the size of your penis?

"You have no idea about my life," I hissed. "Only a person who has walked in someone else's shoes or has tried to see their point of view should be able to analyze or judge someone else. Do you have any idea what I have had to go through in my life? Do you know how it was to grow up as a foreigner wherever I went? Do you know what it's like to have to prove yourself all the time? To women and men? Although they think you're exotic and different, I've had to defend my differentness all my life.

"And now you come along and tell me that I'm too defensive. How dare you come and tell me that? You say that because you never had to defend yourself. I grew up as a French girl in Iran and then a Persian girl in France. At the age of ten I was faced with questions about my nationality and religion."

I stopped and tried to calm down.

"You're just too tense," he replied. "Stop being so defensive."

That was it. My anger just burst out of me.

"Do you know what it's like to grow up among five older male cousins as the only girl and being called the 'French kid' by your own relatives?" I yelled at him, "and then moving to a country where you think, *Alright, now I'll be welcomed.* Of course, you get there and you're a foreigner again. This time it's not because of the language you speak at home or the clothes you wear, but simply because of your different looks and your blood. Your every move and action is examined under a magnifying glass. You stand there as a kid and have to defend your Frenchness to the Iranians and the Iranian roots to the French."

After I started yelling, he got somewhat scared and worried. I must have had this crazy look on my face.

Everyone has a past they are trying to escape. I know he's haunted by his screwed-up marriage and his ex-wife, who was and still is an alcoholic. Now I know what drove her into the world of the bottle—escaping him. He mentioned that he had been with the same woman for twenty-five years. I think now all he thinks about is getting a woman in his bed and making up for lost time.

So what's he worried about? Collecting your damn trophies?

Maybe you would add more to your horde, if you realized that most women are built differently than men when it comes to sexuality and emotions? It's not so separate as it is in a male mind? (I'm not talking about the newer generation who grew up with women's rights, but my generation who inherited those rights and had to learn to juggle them.)

He doesn't know how it is to fear standing alone or defending all the time. He doesn't care that I have no one to fall back on or catch me when I fall.

As I drove home, I was still shaking. I'm not sure if it's because of what he had said or the imbalance it caused in my mind.

You see, this is the same guy who told to me last week, "Where did you come from? It's like you appeared out of nowhere just for me." He told me that he enjoyed cooking for me. He said he liked me. What are these lies? Why did they escape his lips so easily? Why play these games?

Did I lie? Did I play games? I don't think so! As far as I remember, I was honest. I thought I knew him, I had fun talking to him and believed that he understood me. And even if we didn't have a connection, does that give him the right to be so nasty? I'm such an idiot!

October 25, 2006

Amir and I have decided to get a divorce. I just can't take it anymore. His whole existence is irritating me. I'm not sure why we waited for so long. We've been separated for so long, so why not take the last step? I think I was scared and he was scared. I don't know. I think change can be intimidating.

In the end basically after living physically separated, everything will be probably fine, but for now it's scary. I mentioned earlier about reading about the Lewis model of change. It's very interesting. It said that people's lives or habits are like an ice block. They're frozen into a certain shape. To have a successfully change, you have to melt, deciding which parts to keep and how to refreeze into the new shape. The toughest part is defreezing. I don't remember where I first read about the Lewis model, but I apply it to nearly everything now.

Amir and I knew early on that we weren't meant to be. But somehow, the memory kept us afloat. I guess that isn't enough.

We're just too different. When I talk to other women, they say that they have their differences with their spouses. But the question is how much difference is too much? When is it just not worth it anymore? When do you decide this marriage is broken from all the earthquakes, and I just don't have the energy to work on it again and see it crumble for the millionth time?

Of course, there's also the aspect of having children. At the moment, I feel liberated, confused, and somewhat nervous because even though it's what's best for me, I feel like a complete failure as a mother. Lili and Yasmin seem to be fine; I tried talking to them, but they changed the subject. I'm not sure if that's a good or bad sign.

I haven't told any of my friends yet. I think it's better to wait until the announcement. People always treat a separation or divorce like a complete negative phase of your life. Sure, a separation or divorce is nothing to celebrate—well, that's not entirely a bad idea either—but what bugs me is their fucking advice. I just don't want to hear from people who are as unhappy as I was about how I should live my life. I just hate double standards. For example, if Laura wanted to give me advice about how to keep a man happy, I just might die! Come on! Your own guy screws his secretary, and now you want to play Dr. Laura's marriage counseling? Give me a break!

I just have to look at it this way: Everything has to come to an end.

I haven't told the full story to my parents yet. You know how my mom is—she worries too much.

November 3, 2006

Today was Election Day. I'm still interested to know how many women actually take advantage of this day. I guess many younger women take it for granted that they have this right because in many other places they wouldn't have the opportunity to be politically heard. They also don't realize how hard many women before them worked and fought to get us this political power. (And I'm not talking about the 1960s movement for sexual freedom.)

I'm not sure why in 2006 many women think their voice doesn't count and they aren't able to change anything in this big bad world. Do they understand that sometimes the outcome of an election depends on a single vote? Do they realize that if everyone thought like that, we would live in complete chaos?

Getting back to my first point, what really pisses me off is that so many women nearly sacrificed their lives because of their political passion just to be heard, but we all take it for what it is. It's like returning someone's gift. Somehow, I think women like Alice Paul or later Virginia Woolf would climb out of their graves and shake women today. They would tell us how much they did to give us this right and that we should take advantage of it.

Yes, I know progress has been made. We have women in higher political positions but just look at the news. They're still a rarity—and that small percentage of women, who do have the interest and passion for politics, don't even make it to the top as easily as their male counterparts. I wonder why. As women we could actually take that passion, combine it with our emotional side, and use it to our advantage. We don't have to look at all our female characteristics as weaknesses. Instead of pushing our femininity away, we should embrace it. It's so sad that we don't.

I'm curious to see the election results. I wonder if I could check somewhere the ratio of women to men voters.

November 6, 2006

Today I had to bring both kids to the dentist after work. It was such a fiasco. All the x-rays had to be done, and because we had time—yeah, a working mom has time; that's good joke, huh?—he mentioned that some of their cavities should be filled immediately. I figured at least I wouldn't need to come back.

I was sitting in the waiting room, looking through some magazines and answering some e-mails when a father walked in with his two kids. I thought he looked familiar. It turns out that I was right. We had met at one of Julia's barbeques—I'm not sure but it was probably four years ago. We had a very brief introduction, but it had been enough to make an impression. I guess he recognized me as well because he smiled and nodded. When his kids were called into the dentist's office, we were alone in the waiting room and so naturally, we started talking.

One topic led to another, and we said that we would stay in touch, mostly because it seemed that our kids knew each other from school as well. He's involved in some sort of charity work at a hospital, which I thought was very interesting. They were trying to build their Web site and needed someone who was artistic to help with the layout. I told him I would love to help out!

His name is Michael.

November 7, 2006

So I decided to help with the charity organization at the hospital after work. It was a blood collection, so it was for a good cause. Doing charity work makes you feel wonderful. Besides, if I want to help set-up a Web site, I should know some of the people I'm working for so I can ask them questions about what they want on it and how they want it to work.

It was so cold, and by the end of my shift, my feet were as frozen and pointy as my shoes. When I got home and took my shoes off, I looked at my heels and noticed that they get higher each year. It's one way I can always stay taller than my kids and be a mother they can look up to. I wonder who invented high heel shoes for women. Marilyn Monroe said, "I don't know who invented high heels, but all women owe him a lot." I agree with her. Not only do I like that they make me walk higher, but also I love the way I walk in them. My weight and balance is completely different.

It might also be that we like higher heels because we automatically—regardless of the appearance of fragility—behave differently in them. I feel as if I'm a goddess up on high. And then there are the moments when I break a heel and come plummeting back to reality—ugh, it still pisses me off when I think about that Prada heel.

But then again, women can't run as fast in heels, and they make us look more fragile and delicate. I think that's what men like most about those shoes. It's not only how our butt moves as we're trying to not fall down.

Once I did a little test. I went into the same store twice in two different types of shoes—once in flats and once in heels. Guess what? They treated me differently. Don't laugh because it's true. Something about the flats made me feel—shorter, more girlish, and less arrogant.

Well, I guess the blood collectors didn't really care about my heels, but it felt good when an older woman, who was smiling at me, said, "Oh my, I used to wear those kinds of shoes when I was young. Enjoy it, dear."

Well, I do.

November 10, 2010

I had an e-mail from Michael today. It wasn't about anything in particular. He just wanted to say hi, which led to a thirty-minute phone conversation. He thanked me for helping out the other day and asked about my work. Suddenly we were talking about the last books we had read and about our favorite restaurants and music. It was a very personal conversation but on a nonsexual level.

Maybe I'm reading too much into this, but I compare it to the fiascos with the other men I met this year: Steven, Ben, and Paul. They were only interested in one topic and not serious in-depth conversations. There was no talk about kids and literature, law and politics, culture and history, or music and art. To give Paul the benefit- I did have some nice conversations with him. But they were rather a "defend your opinion" than an opinion exchange. Remember how he started attacking me because of my bi-cultural background, instead of asking questions about how it felt to be in a split position between two completely different cultures. How I felt not only as a woman, but as a human in general to be French-Iranian? He would say something against French or Iranian people just to see which one I defended more.

All these years I've been searching for someone who would understand me, be on my emotional level, still stimulate me mentally, respectfully challenge my opinions, and treat me as an equal. All these years, I was looking for my so-called "lost" half, the one who would complete me. Someone I didn't have to fight, who would look beyond physical attraction and who saw me as an entire person, body, and soul. It doesn't matter how long you know a person; if he's the one who you're supposed to meet, you'll notice each other. Your thoughts work in the same manner, and you feel the same about many issues. When he says something, you can finish the sentence he started. You don't have to pretend and invent Giselle. You notice the person is happy just to hear your voice or e-mails you to say hi.

At home, the kids are getting ready for their exams. It's so tense. Each one is moaning about all the work: their assignments, projects, and you name it. Sometimes I wonder why so many teachers just seem to dump all this work on them. Yeah, I understand, it is the curriculum, and we have to reach a certain standard to keep our children, who will be tomorrow's workforce, globally competitive. But is the solution to burn them out with information and facts before they've reached the age of twenty? Wouldn't we rather filter out what information won't be useful for them in the practical world?

I don't know that it has to be all about information as well. Sometimes awareness is just as important. We should teach them that not every child has the privileges they do: They can't go to school, have their own room, or go constantly to the mall. They need to know that there are children in our twenty-first century who actually have to work hard for money and would love to buy a book or have new clothes instead of someone's hand-me-downs.

I always feel that all of these book-smart kids would be somewhat lost in the real world. Their awakening usually comes after they start their first job or pay their first month of rent.

You know what? This is also something I can discuss with Michael.

November 17, 2006

It's been a full week of e-mails and phone calls. I can't believe it. If anyone reads this, he or she would think I'm sick. I think the same thing. I mean the guy is married for heaven's sake! I know it, and he knows it. And nothing has happened or will ever happen between the two of us.

But Michael makes me feel so good. I enjoy talking to him; I talk to him about all kinds of things: about the divorce, my kids, his kids, life in general, and you name it. He's such a tough businessperson on the outside, but in front of me, he's so sweet.

If anyone ever asked me why I like him so much—okay, *too* much—I could give them a long list of why's matched up with a longer list of why I shouldn't even think about him: He blushes every time he sees me; he smiles when I enter the room; he's so interested in everything I do and say; when he thinks I'm not looking, he's always staring at me—just listen to me, I sound like a lovestruck teenager—when he phones me, he calls me his favorite girl; and when I joke with him and tease him by instant message, which he told me he receives sometimes during meetings, he starts smiling automatically.

He called me tonight, and we talked for about an hour. The girls were at the movies with friends, Amir was still at work, so I had the whole house to myself.

"We should be careful," he cautioned. "If we aren't, we will slowly cross a line that won't end well for either of us."

"I agree," I replied, but I wasn't about to hang up.

"The first time I saw you," he said with a laugh, "I felt so attracted to you, and I still am. I have thousands of reasons for liking you."

"But the fact is that we're both at a stage in our lives that doesn't allow us to cross that line. You'll always make me smile and blush, and it feels so good to talk to you. Oh man, the entire timing of this is so unfair and sad."

I agreed with him, but I didn't say anything though. What could I say? He's right; it's all so unfair and sad.

"I'm a married man—a happily married," he commented.

I thought, *I know you're married, but I don't believe the "happy part." If you were happy, you wouldn't call me or send me e-mails.* But that's a different issue and doesn't matter. The fact is he *is* married.

"I won't e-mail, text, or call you anymore," I said, doing what any woman with some brains should do.

He was quiet for a while and then said, "I doubt that."

"No, I'm very stubborn; if you're also happily married, you shouldn't care."

Then he was quiet.

"What happened? Are you still there?" I asked.

He made a little noise on the other end of the line.

"Will you miss me?" I inquired. "Will you be sad?"

"Extremely sad."

Then there was complete silence.

"Michael? Are you still there?"

It was quiet. I called his name again, and then I realized that he was crying. I heard a sigh on the other side of the line.

"If you were a girl, I would ask you if you were crying."

He laughed a sad laugh, and then it was very quiet again.

"I have been known to make some men cry."

"I'll be extremely said if I don't hear from you anymore," he confessed.

Look, I have to be rational; the guy is married! I keep saying to myself. *I don't want to be a home wrecker. It doesn't matter whether he is happy or not. The fact is he's married.*

We talked some more about relationships, houses, kids, and education, and then I had to leave and so did he.

"Then I shouldn't talk to you anymore?"

"No," I replied. "I think it's for the best. Don't worry. I'll be fine."

I tried to laugh it off as we said good-bye.

When I hung up, I realized just how much I already missed his voice—so much so that I believed my heart was beating too quickly at once, like pre-mature cardiac contractions. I was the one who had suggested not calling or talking. I've said this to a lot of men, but I've rarely felt this way.

I tried to get him out of my brain, by keeping myself busy with the thousand things in my crazy life. But how can I take him out of my heart? I know I've just known him for a short time, but he has become part of my life. I look forward to his calling me or sending me a text. I get excited when I hear the excitement and nervousness in his voice when he calls me. When I send him e-mails that might be somewhat provocative, I literally feel how and when he smiles and blushes.

I had once read in a book—I think it was by Paulo Coelho—about love. The Greeks used to say that men and women were attached at their spines. Spouses kept their mate with them, they used to do everything together, and they knew each other like no one else would ever know them. When the gods saw this, they got upset and jealous. They asked Zeus to separate the couples because humans were able to accomplish more and didn't have to look for their compatible match. Zeus did what he was asked to do and separated men and women. Ever since then, men and women feel lost and are looking for their mates, not knowing who is the one with whom their soul should be paired.

That's exactly how I feel now. Even after such a short time, I feel that kind of connection with Michael, and the fact that he expressed the same sentiment doesn't make it easier for me. But I have to stay away from him.

It's so difficult. I know when I go to work on Monday, I will feel empty because I'm not receiving e-mails or texts from him, and I have to control myself, not getting lost in my feelings and emotions.

I can't be friends with him; I think I truly fell in love with him—and he's with another woman. It's so unfair, sad, and unreasonable. You can call it anything you want. Why did I have to meet him now? Why now?

Sometimes I wish I could have had one day alone with him. I just wanted to hold him, be held by him, fall asleep in his arms, and wake up with him next to me, smiling. I want to see him laugh, touch him, be touched by him, and have him feel me.

Only once before have I mentally opened up to man and felt as though I don't have to pretend to be someone else. I didn't have to be Giselle or anyone else. I could be *me*. Oh, it's so unfair. But I'm doing the right thing even though it's breaking my heart.

November 20, 2006

No e-mails. No calls. Silence.

I feel so empty, but I have to be strong. My heart hurts. I feel lost. I cried at my desk and had to make sure no one saw.

I miss him, and I can't tell him how much. ☹

The kids know that something isn't right with me. They were also quiet. I guess there's still a very strong psychological umbilical cord between us.

November 25, 2006

Okay, first let me give you the pre-story: I was invited to a very posh Thanksgiving party at Amy's, and of course, because it was right after the elections, everyone was talking politics. And, although I had promised to *never, never* get involved in political conversations at parties, it still happened. (Years ago I was insulted by a young kid [okay, he was twenty, but mentally probably two] for being French, liberal, supporting the poor, and mostly being me.) So I told myself, *Never again.* I limited the shut-up approach to mostly when I'm at a party where I don't know people's opinions. Some people can't respect someone else's thoughts and use insults as their defense instead of building their own arguments.

Anyway, I was looking for a friend, who was talking to a guest. She introduced me to her conversation partner. I faced this attractive gray-haired gentleman; judging from his appearance, he was well educated and came from a good family. He introduced himself and after the normal greetings, our common friend mentioned that I worked as a graphic artist and was very liberal, the kind of comments you make before the conversation becomes embarrassingly quiet. But this time it was different. This man—I forgot his name—said laughingly that he would never agree with my political opinions, but that my field of work always produced people like me. I chuckled and launched back. Now you can imagine that there was more roasting that evening than just the turkey in the oven. Our arguments flew back and forth like a ball in a tennis match—but in a respectful manner. There was no fist fighting—until later on in the conversation when I mentioned that I believed in class equality, not the pyramid system that our society has created.

That wasn't a big deal, right? The fact that I was dressed up, while saying this seemed to challenge him! He commented on my attire, and I started. *Huh? What does my appearance have to do anything with my political opinion?* I thought. I grew up in a socialist country, where we believed that no matter how much you made, you kept enough for yourself and gave the rest to the ones who weren't as lucky as you. Unlike communism, socialism doesn't require that you give everything away. I have a certain budget and have enough for myself; however, I give about a third or sometimes even half of my income to charities.

What I don't understand is why someone after the party approached me and said, "How can you say that you believe in equality? If you did, you wouldn't drive a fancy car and live in a fancy place."

This was someone who had no idea what my ideology in life is and what I do with my money. It was someone who ignorantly believed that you have to walk around unwashed to *show* that you're a liberal or you care. They're probably the same people who think that a woman who looks good can't think at the same time or if you believe in capitalism, you have money growing on trees in your backyard! What does the outside have to do with the inside? If I showed everyone what I did, wouldn't it be prideful? Instead, I like to give and help quietly. It's like those people who believe that you can't be a Muslim if you aren't wearing a burka or praying in front of people.

Now in defense of that person's ignorance, I have to say that many people still think this way, which is a shame. Look sometimes you might work in a certain environment where you're "forced" to dress in a specific manner and are expected to have a certain appearance. Then your clothes make you the person that society wants you to be, but that should never change your beliefs. There's no dressing to showcase political affiliation, but there's acting with political belief, which can shape how you dress!

The kids loved the party by the way. Both of them enjoy Thanksgiving regardless of the turkey's affiliation.

December 1, 2006

I don't know why I'm recently thinking so much about God. I miss his/her presence.

December 2, 2006

I'm all mixed up right now, and you won't believe why. I just passed my bathroom, which was formerly Amir's and mine, and Amir was in there. He had probably had forgotten something because he hasn't moved all of his stuff out yet. He was shaving, and just watching him shave was such a turn-on. Don't laugh, but there's something so intimate about how a man actually takes time and looks at—no examines— his face in a mirror, slowly puts the shaving cream on, and glides the razor through those little mountains of foam. It's so sexy how strike by strike his face slowly becomes visible again and only small lines of white are witnesses of the change.

Anyway, I'm all confused because of this five-minute scene. He didn't notice that I was watching him, but it brought back memories. The closer his move out gets, the more I think about what we could have, should have, and might have been able to have had if we were to try again. But then, I remember all the fighting and yelling—I'm not sure what I'm doing. Is it right to end this entire relationship? When does a woman know it's over? I know, I sound like a broken record, but things change, people change, and relationships change. Maybe we're just not willing to accept it. Maybe we were both too stubborn to see what we each had to change to be together.

I guess it's normal to have those doubts right before a divorce. I mean, no one understands it unless they have gone through it. Now, there are those situations where physical abuse or adultery is involved, and those are the angry divorces. The screaming, fighting, and yelling continues up until to the court date. But some divorces are different; it's called "amicable." Just what the fuck does that mean? Either you get along or you don't. I guess it means that we won't fighting over life's every little detail after the break. But if we can get along, then why are we breaking it off? Because we were fighting all the time—it's an ongoing circle.

Why is it that sometimes the best friends make the worst spouses or the worst spouses make the best friends? Amir and I used to get along beautifully as friends. We were so different, but we complimented each other and shared some good laughter- all before we were married. He even watched a couple of chick-flick movies with me. And I sat through an entire baseball game. Why then and not now? Because back then we were not obliged to get along, each one could leave to their own place when they got tired of the other one. Is marriage supposed to be based on friendship or attraction? Why are we sometimes attracted to the wrong person? So many questions are storming through my mind and unfortunately they don't connect and don't lead me to an answer.

Don't they always say that the female intuitively chooses the best father for the kids? But then why do we choose the wrong guy? If I'm judging based on attraction, research shows that all five senses are usually used to select the appropriate mate. But then why don't I get along with that person? The research must be wrong. It can't be *just* the five senses. Of course, I have a couple of very dear male friends, with who I always get along, but could never imagine having sex with or marrying. I'm just not attracted to them. I guess it must be some weird sort of combination of all. But is it friendship first and then attraction or attraction first and then friendship? Oh, this all is so complicated.

Based on that we should be like animals, or do animals divorce? I haven't met a canine divorce lawyer yet, but maybe I should look into this—not the lawyer, I mean whether animals divorce.

Oh, look at me again, just one five-minute incident brings me into a examination of the philosophy of men and women. Enough. Good night!

December 5, 2006

It was my birthday; I turned thirty-five, so I'm halfway into my thirties now. I'm not sure why this year is tougher for me to accept than thirty was. When I turned thirty, I felt as if I was still able to be counted with the twenty-year-olds. Now, I'm just jogging—no running—toward forty!

That probably doesn't make sense, I know.

But isn't age just a number? I used to think that for most of my life until you aren't referred to as "Miss" at any counter or when no one ask for your ID when you buy a bottle of wine.

The kids were so sweet; Lili and Yasmin bought me a gift certificate to a spa. Amir asked whether he could take us all out for dinner. I agreed. Somehow, the active war between us isn't as active anymore. I wouldn't say that we're living in perfect peace, but at least we can talk about everyday things while keeping our voices at a reasonable volume and pitch. No yelling here.

In a way, the situation makes me feel empty. I mean we were passionately in love, then we had the biggest fights, then we fell into a cold war by ignoring each other, and now we are just quiet. I was so used to this particular tension for half of my life and now this relaxed stage makes me feel as though something is missing.

Well, anyway, many friends called or sent me e-mails, wishing me Happy Birthday! It is nice that they thought of me.

Michael should be happy, because I still think of him, but I'm glad he didn't send me birthday wishes.

I do wonder how he is.

December 10, 2006

Guess who I saw today? You'll never believe it! It was the Jewish woman from Lisa's party last summer, who spoke fluent French. After all the greeting and blah-blah, she told me that they had a special ceremony at their temple that evening and she would love to invite me. "Sure," I said. "I'll come."

That evening Yasmin and I dressed up and went. Lili went to someone's party. The service was amazing! I had gone to temple before, once for some other thing that I don't even remember. But this time, everyone was so dressed up and formal. The rabbi greeted me and was delighted that a non-Jew would be the Guest of the Day. When he said that to me, I felt so welcomed. I got tears in my eyes. It didn't matter which praying house I was at—they're all the same, I have never been too religious, but somehow the whole atmosphere and his warm words made me feel connected.

I remember my grandmother always verbally bashed Jews. Plus, after watching the way now Christians, Jews, and Muslim treat each other, I just have never seen what's the big deal. They are all in their own boxes, convinced that what they said and practiced was right and the God they worshiped was the "One." Honestly, who cares? Don't they all say the same thing: Don't kill, don't steal, and don't cheat? But then their so-called worshippers do all of the above. They go into their churches, mosques, or temples; say, "Yes!" and, "Amen!" to everything their rabbis, imams, and priests say; and as soon as they come out, the words they said roll of their skins like water off a duck's back, having fallen on deaf ears.

The whole atmosphere made me realize even more how similar all these religions are—in their wrong practices. Sure, there are small differences, like pray this time of the day and don't eat this, etc. These differences are like all the shirts in your closet: one blue, one green, one linen, and the other silk. They all have one thing in common: They are all shirts that cover most of the upper part of your body. I don't think you have to keep them separate in your closet. (Well, I admit I hang mine by their colors, which makes it easier to pull them out in the morning.) There's no battle in your closet with one saying it looks nicer or is better, just because it has a designer label on the inside and the other one answering, "No, but I have this fashionable color." So tell me why do humans, who claim that they are the highest-functioning of the creatures on earth, fight and kill each other just because each group thinks that the way they praise their God is the only true way? Shouldn't we all look at the common denominator instead of the small differences?

I mean, shouldn't religion be about doing good, having respect, and not killing? Shouldn't it be about how to think about your common man? Regardless of what people say, I believe that there was the same creator for each one of the groups! Plus, you can't convince me that a man who kills another because that person is of a different religion is thinking about his God in that moment. He is just thinking about his own power by proving that he is right and the other one is wrong. Religion should bring people closer, but unfortunately, it kills and pulls people apart. What a shame.

This is the moment, when I think that humans aren't the highest-functioning creature, but the lowest. Although we invent one thing after the next, send people to the moon, fly to Mars, and develop iPhones and flat screens, we are still killing each other in worse ways than in the Animal Kingdom. If you look at history, it starts from the Zoroastrians, who killed the prophet Mani; then went to the

Arabs, who killed Zoroastrians; then goes to the Jews who kill Muslims; and continues on to the Hindus, who think no one outside their caste is pure. What is this? I know it might sound like wishful thinking, but why do you have to kill someone for the way they worship their God? Is there a rulebook for what is right and wrong? Shouldn't that be a very personal matter? When I start to think about these question, I truly believe that religion isn't the belief of a person, but the force of separation and the force to kill.

But the warm welcome today at the temple does give me some hope. I just hope that one day all people with different believes can focus more on the common denumerator of the religions. That all of them are willing to accept their similarities they might be able to find a way to

December 11, 2006

Today my school friend Maria called me. I didn't recognize her voice because I hadn't spoken to her in more than a year. After the usual chitchat, she told me that she did get divorced. I told her that I had no idea there had been trouble in their marriage. She said that she had been a good actor and had been faking it all these years. Her reason for the divorce: her mother-in-law. I was surprised, but then after I thought about it, it made sense. Then she opened up and told me more about what had happened.

When he was a teenager some thirty years ago, Lou, her ex-husband, had moved to the States with his entire family. The father had been abusive, and of course, as their only child, he felt responsible to protect his mom. I guess I understand the bond Lou and his mother had, being immigrants to a foreign country. When Lou met Maria, he wanted to have his mother live with them, but Maria made it clear from the beginning that she was only going to marry Lou and not his mother. She had wanted some privacy as a new bride. I understand her completely even though I do empathize with the mother as well. Imagine when Maria and Lou would have wanted to be intimate, his mother would be next door. That's totally awkward. Lou's mother was still young and didn't need any physical care so why not keep her own dignity and move out? Maria and Lou were married for five years and I still laugh at what brought the final cut to their marriage. It is one of those incidents where you are so shocked that you just start laughing. She just could not take it anymore after her mother-in-law walked into their bedroom while they were having sex. "You guys should stop that now! You have done it five times this week." You know, I love my daughters more than anything in this world—they are the best things that have ever happened to me—but I would never want to move in with them when they are older. Generations should be separate but not forgotten.

As I listened to Maria's story, I remembered when my soon-to-be ex–mother-in-law had the same expectations of living with us and making the decisions in my home. As a new bride, it's really important for a young woman to make even the smallest decisions for her household. She wants to be the one to decide which flowers should be on the table and what they should have for dinner. (I do know some generations who do live together, and it seems to be working fine, but I think those are rare cases.) And just imagine when grandchildren arrive. Although it's good to have someone to watch the kids, so you can work or even go out once in a while, how do you maintain your authority over the kids? Shouldn't the parents determine the child's upbringing? I don't know. All in all the idea of having different generations bothers me a lot.

As far as Maria's situation, I wondered why on earth Lou's mom wanted to live with her son and his wife? Usually these mothers-in-law didn't have happy marriages, and their sons are usually the only children. These women see them as the ideal husbands they would have loved to have. Basically, they were able to raise and "make" the ideal man. Now the time has come for these ideal men to start a new relationship with women who aren't them. They can't handle it. Their adoration makes them unable to let go. It's sickening.

The sad thing is now that Maria and Lou are divorced, Lou's mother has a free pass to move in. I'm sure she'll be disappointed because she'll want it to be as it was, not realizing that meanwhile her son has been through a marriage, separation, and divorce and, hence, has been shaped and changed by that relationship. It's ironic and usually this is usually the part the mother figures out too late.

December 14, 2006

I read a book about religion in general. I told you that recently I have been thinking a lot about God, and I guess the temple visit brought it to the forefront. Sure, I was raised with a faith. (There's nothing wrong with being in a family without one.) At times I forget about the "last door," as I like to call prayers. Don't we usually turn around and ask in moments of desperation when we're looking for answers from a higher power?

So what does that mean for me? When was the last time I really spoke to my God? I mean not the Oh-my-God-hello-it's-me talk but really talking, telling him once in a while how I'm truly thankful for everything he has given me. Sure, I think that my life sucks at times. But there's a balance, right? It couldn't be that he gave me the short end of everything and forgot about me when he distributed luck.

Sure, my marriage didn't turn out the way I wanted. But without that marriage, I wouldn't have had my girls. Maybe I wasn't supposed to stay with Amir forever but just be with him to create these two kids. Maybe these two girls are supposed to do something special down the road, which wouldn't have happened without my marriage. I mean what if what happened yesterday shapes what happens tomorrow and the day after, a sort of cosmic pre-step to good.

In the end, I think somebody up there loves me, no matter what you call him.

December 24, 2006

What a wonderful Christmas Eve we had! Even though Amir and I knew our ceasefire held for only this evening, both of us realized that this was our last Christmas together. My, how memories bind people. Fifteen years ago I met him on Christmas, and now we celebrated our sixteenth anniversary of knowing each other and our last Christmas together. It all feels very sentimental. I made a Christmas duck with all the veggies, which the kids love. We had Bûche de Noël and just sat by the fire. Like we always have, we played board games and then watched a movie after reading *Auntie Claus*, which is such lovely story. Every year we all notice new things about it.

Even though they are teenagers, the kids were so excited this year—normally you wouldn't expect this level of excitement about anything. They simply loved all their gifts. They were so happy for each other as well. It was so peaceful. Just thinking about the entire evening makes me cry.

At the end of the night, Amir hugged me, kissed my cheek, and said that I was a great mother. I guess that's all I can ask for. It was the *best* gift of all.

December 31, 2006

Well, this is the last time I'm writing this year. Every year I like to look back at what I wrote on December 31 of the previous year and see whether everything on this year's to-do list was checked off. This year I won't. I actually reread my whole diary and saw all the changes in my life through the 83 entries. I would have never imagined that so many things would occur and change in my life. It's really true when they say that we are sometimes too impatient. Everything really happens for a reason, and if we were just more tolerant and patient, it ends up for the best.

My girls are growing into beautiful young ladies, both with their own ideas about life. They are thinking about their own future, and although it includes me, I'll have to accept that I can only take the role of an observer—unless they ask me for advice, which I will be honored to give. I have to stand back and let them make their own mistakes. I have to give them wings to fly away— but make sure that they know that they can always fly back to me. Through Lili and Yasmin, I learned to live in all three tenses: the past (I still see them as babies, completely helpless and lying in my arms), future (the young women they'll be as they go and live their own lives), and most importantly the present (enjoying what they are this very moment because in the next blink of an eye, it'll be a memory).

I learned in those four months of unemployment, that I can only make those around me happy if I'm happy myself. As trivial as it sounds, I don't think a lot of women are aware of that. We want to give up everything: First, we live under our parents' rules, then we give up most of that freedom for the man we love, and then we hand over what's left to our children. This mentality is in every woman, not just a typical

Middle Eastern one. We truly love to sacrifice of ourselves, only making those around us happy even though we might be miserable ourselves. I don't think that's right.

I've a right to my own existence as well. Although I'm a daughter, companion, mother, friend, and everything else I choose to be, I think at least ten percent of my existence should belong to *me*. I have to be happy to make those around me smile. That's the internal balance.

I also learned about love—after the divorce. What a bad timing! I always looked for someone who would, in a way, put me on a pedestal and worship me as his woman. Not anymore. Sure, I'm a woman and love to be worshiped like a personal goddess. I think Sophia Loren might have said this. But then on Christmas Eve, as Lili, Yasmin, Amir, and I reread *Auntie Claus*, which I had given the girls when they were little, I realized that every one of us is like that little girl in the story. We always take the simple things for granted. All that little girl wanted was gifts for herself—until she had to learn how bad it made her feel when she got something and her little brother got nothing. That's when I realized how much we take being loved for granted. I don't necessarily want to be only the loved one, but I want to give my love as well and make sure that the people I'm with know what they mean to me. Giving is as important as receiving this love. Yes, I'm still headstrong and emancipated, but I think it's fine when I can also spoil a man, knowing that he needs me, instead of always protecting myself from loving too much.

I learned something out of every up and down experience from the past 365 days. And although I might not be able to use all this knowledge in the coming year, I'm still happy that I had the opportunity to change and grow, mostly in my value as a woman and becoming aware that only *I* can make my own life.

Happy New Year 2007.